The Wisdom of God

The message of the cross is foolish to those who are headed for destruction! But we who are being saved know it is the very power of God. As the Scriptures say,

> *"I will destroy the wisdom of the wise*
> *and discard the intelligence of the intelligent."*

So where does this leave the philosophers, the scholars, and the world's brilliant debaters? God has made the wisdom of this world look foolish. Since God in his wisdom saw to it that the world would never know him through human wisdom, he has used our foolish preaching to save those who believe. It is foolish to the Jews, who ask for signs from heaven. And it is foolish to the Greeks, who seek human wisdom. So when we preach that Christ was crucified, the Jews are offended and the Gentiles say it's all nonsense.

> *But to those called by God to salvation, both Jews and Gentiles,*
> *Christ is the power of God and the wisdom of God.*

> *~ 1 Corinthians 1:18-24 ~*

i

Book Reviews

Crisis of Belief describes the narrow path that God has led James down. Few find that path. Fewer stay on it. Fewer yet find the courage to speak of those lessons or dare to put them into written words. James' personal story provides a lot of signs, lessons learned, and bread crumbs that you can pick up and apply to your own life. God's blessings, His patience, and His mercy show up in many different and unexpected ways once we take the time to look, to listen, and to wait. My prayer is that others would open this book's pages and absorb the compassion of God waiting for them within.

~ *Clark Jacobson*

James Timothy Butt's *Crisis of Belief* should be a movie! Many are called, but few are chosen. Few are there who desire Papa God's Heart so desperately that they go above and beyond being Jesus' friends and followers, to actually become His disciples. Jesus' teachings offended some of His followers, and so some of them turned back. Not many dare to risk everything to be a disciple of Jesus, but James Timothy Butt paid the expensive price, he paid it all. *Crisis of Belief* is one of those beloved "could not put the book down" autobiographies.

~ *Linda Bartlett, Author; "Hellbound: A Love Story"*

While reading *Crisis of Belief,* thoughts were swirling in my head and in my heart which at times were overwhelming since this book reminded me of issues from my past, both as a child and an adult. James' candid sharing of his walk with God challenges the reader to examine their own walk. It is my hope that this book inspires you to choose the narrow path, to accept it's challenges, and to persist through your own "crises of belief" until the day you bow before His throne to hear those words, "Well done, thou good and faithful servant." Great book. I highly recommend it!!!!

~ *Susan Hopkins Randolph*

"God's timing is always perfect. It is never early, but it is always exactly on time." This excerpt from James' book (among others) spoke to me as if it were coming straight from God sitting at my breakfast table. James' candid testimonies of his ever-changing, wild, exciting, and sometimes painful journey of faith make his readers want to experience the same intense and rewarding relationship with God that he has.

~ *Christie White*

This book is an open and honest chronicle displaying God's amazing grace which empowers a person to forsake all and follow Christ. It both challenges and motivates the reader to find the narrow way and it encourages us to stay the course. What initially appears as a *crisis of belief* to us is really an open door from God inviting us into richer experiences with Jesus which we can't find any other way. By persevering along the narrow path we see just how faithful our God really is and we learn that overcoming is a reward in itself. This book captivates the reader's attention until the very end.

~ Kim Combs

A gripping life story with no-holds-barred. His story of total abandonment of all things to the Lord in pursuit of Him is inspirational to those of us who seek undiluted love; love with no bounds and with everything we are.

~ Dora Wang

Crisis of Belief is absolutely inspirational and filled with the Holy Spirit. James is a genuine Christ follower and disciple. I shared this book with two people who were greatly appreciative.

~ Luiz Godinho
Musician, Renew Church, Milton, ON, Canada

I began reading James' book the moment I received it, read it straight through lunch, and just finished it near the end of the day. The book is a perfect example of how our God makes beauty from ashes. So much of what James says is VERY applicable to so many who wish to be followers of Jesus.

~ Chaplain Michael Tummillo

Crisis of Belief provides the reader with a sense of relief that his or her trials are not uncommon to man. James' transparency and raw storytelling will keep you engaged and provoke you to gaze back at the cross. It gave me fresh faith for what God can do in my own life!

~ Elizabeth Mello

When I heard that Jimmy Butt had "found religion," I wondered if God had answered my prayers long forgotten since high school, and He did! Not only had Jimmy gotten saved, he'd written a book about it! When I got his book I couldn't put it down, nor could I believe what I was reading! Not only had God rescued Jim, he had dramatically changed him!

~ Linda Sottile Douglas

A wonderful read and a challenging book, *Crisis of Belief; The Narrow Path that Few Follow* is a call to action for all Christians; especially American believers so blessed with so much, yet living in a time of hyper-grace and a watered-down gospel. Perfectly aligned with sound doctrine, it resets the shaken moral compass of today's church! James learned to walk by the leading of the Holy Spirit and not common sense. Many *crises of belief* trials were used as his training ground to prepare him like a good soldier for his next task! His entire personal testimony is peppered with scripture references! In conclusion, I would highly recommend this book. It has moved, affected, and inspired me to press on in my own walk with my Lord!

~ Beth Bumbier

James Butt's *Crisis of Belief* is raw, captivating, convicting, moving, and strongly written with humility of a journey from "free will" to His marvelous light. I would recommend sharing this book with as many who are in a crisis.

~ Mary Ann Ontiveros

Autobiographies written with the goal of giving God the glory are more interesting than fiction or autobiographies written as bragging rights. I read James' book in two nights. His transparency and humility point to the saving grace of Jesus Christ of Nazareth. Knowing him personally, I see he is walking in a rich generational inheritance with treasures yet to unfold. Quite a journey and quite a life. Looking forward to reading the unwritten chapters as the best is yet to come.

~ Jennifer Dixon

With God's strength, and supernatural guidance, James breaks free of overwhelming addictions and then he leaves behind everything to live a passionate and courageous life for Christ. His account is both captivating and life-changing. James testimony reveals a loving and powerful God who does the impossible in and through him making a difference in many lives. If you are serious with your walk with God, I am confident that as you read *Crisis of Belief* you will grow in faith and be inspired to live a more passionate and committed life to God.

~ Bruce Koch

Special Appreciation

Cover Image, book design: *Therese L. Spina MFA*
Therese Spina Ltd. https://www.facebook.com/theresespinaltd

Website: *Steffi Ewing, Global Village*

Editors, 2nd Edition: *Pastor Laura Berndt, Therese Spina MFA*

Book Foreword, 2nd Edition: *Pastor Juliet Canhu*

Book Foreword from 1st Edition, Revised: *Pastor Laura Berndt*

Special Contributors: *Dora Wang & Wade Ferris*
Thank you, Dora for your help with the Self-Reflection Questions!
Thank you, Wade for your support which helped to make this book possible!

Crisis of Belief

The Narrow Path that Few Follow

By James Timothy Butt

Foreword by
Juliet Canha

And they have defeated him by the blood of the Lamb
and by their testimony.
And they did not love their lives so much
that they were afraid to die.
~ Revelation 12:11~

Crisis of Belief—The Narrow Path That Few Follow
By James Timothy Butt

This work is dedicated to the public domain
for the glory of God and His kingdom!!!

This book, in print or downloadable form, with the exception of the front image by Therese Spina Ltd., may be printed, reproduced, or distributed freely in any form by any means–electronic, mechanical, photocopy, or otherwise - without prior written permission.

Second Edition

This book is available for purchase at amazon.com
and as a free download at CrisisofBelief.com

Cover Image, book design: Therese L. Spina MFA
Therese Spina Ltd. https://www.facebook.com/theresespinaltd

Website: Steffi Ewing Global Village

Crisis of Belief

I waited patiently for the LORD to help me,
and he turned to me and heard my cry.
He lifted me out of the pit of despair,
out of the mud and the mire.
He set my feet on solid ground
and steadied me as I walked along.
He has given me a new song to sing,
a hymn of praise to our God.
Many will see what he has done and be amazed.
They will put their trust in the LORD.
Oh, the joys of those who trust the LORD,
who have no confidence in the proud
or in those who worship idols.
O LORD my God, you have performed many wonders for us.
Your plans for us are too numerous to list. You have no equal.
If I tried to recite all your wonderful deeds
I would never come to the end of them.
You take no delight in sacrifices or offerings.
Now that you have made me listen, I finally understand—
you don't require burnt offerings or sin offerings.
Then I said, "Look, I have come.
As it is written about me in the Scriptures:
I take joy in doing your will, my God,
for your instructions are written on my heart."
I have told all your people about your justice.
I have not been afraid to speak out,
as you, O LORD, well know.
I have not kept the good news of your justice hidden in my heart;
I have talked about your faithfulness and saving power.
I have told everyone in the great assembly
of your unfailing love and faithfulness.
LORD, don't hold back your tender mercies from me.
Let your unfailing love and faithfulness always protect me.

~ Psalm 40:1–11~

Table of Contents

Front Matter .... i-ix

Foreword 1

Foreword to the First Edition 2

Introduction 4

Becoming "Born Again" 11

1. Is That All There Is? 12

2. A Wake-Up Call 16

3. Pain, Healing, and Forgiveness 19

4 . My Failed Marriages 24

5. A Checkup from the Neck Up 28

6. Playing in the Devil's Playground 32

7. Becoming God Conscious 35

8. A New Life 41

9. Learning to Hear God's Voice 45

The Seed Planted in Good Soil 50

10. The Narrow Path that Few Find 51

11. The Spirit Realm 55

12. The Red Tank Top 58

13. The Devil Gets Desperate 63

14. The Best Day of My Life 68

Answering the Call to be Sent 74

15. Signs, Wonders and More Baptisms 75

16. Walk to Emmaus 79

17. Jumping Off the Income Cliff 85

18. Crow Nation—Mission Trip and Bible College .. 89

19. Brotherly Love and Accountability Partners .. 98

20. My "Perfect Job" is Sacrificed 102

Table of Contents

Being Equipped and Crucified *108*

21. The Birthing of a Vision 109

22. Spiritual Gifts 116

23. A Spiritual Father and the Five-fold Ministry 120

24. The Beginning of Unity 124

25. The Power of the Cross Festival 2006 129

26. Producer at Austin Public Access Television 135

27. The Power of the Cross Festival 2007 140

28. Total Reckless Abandon 145

The Ministry of Reconciliation *150*

29. A Place to Rest My Head 151

30. Blooming Where God Plants You 156

31. God Heals Two Women 160

32. Four Divine Appointments—Easter 2009 165

The Fathers Provision *169*

33. Supernatural Grace 170

34. A Head-On Collision with Destiny 175

35. Turns Out I'm No Longer a Salesman 179

The Battle to Advance God's Kingdom *182*

36. The Devil Tried to Destroy Me 183

37. The Kingdom on Earth 188

38. Building the Kingdom 193

39. The Ministry of Reconciliation: Sharing the Good News 199

40. Next Stop, Kansas City 204

Eternal Salvation Prayer *210*

Back Matter 214

For God was in Christ,
reconciling the world to himself,
no longer counting people's sins against them.
And he gave us this wonderful message of reconciliation.

~ 2 Corinthians 5:19 ~

Foreword

There is wonderful joy ahead, even though you must endure many trials
for a little while. These trials will show that your faith is genuine.
It is being tested as fire tests and purifies gold –
though your faith is far more precious than mere gold.
So when your faith remains strong through many trials,
it will bring you much praise and glory and honor
on the day when Jesus Christ is revealed to the whole world.
~ 1 Peter 1:6–7 ~

Have you ever faced a *crisis of belief* on your faith journey of following Jesus? A similar term one might use to describe such a *crisis of belief* is: "a test of faith".

In this autobiography, James shares many of his tests of faith which set him up for several inspired God encounters, resulting in supernatural covenant provision and miracles. A true page-turner, you may find yourself rushing through the story, eager to find out what happens next. I encourage you, however, to take your time to read through it again, the second time to focus on a unique feature in this book; the rich and inspiring scripture references at the end of each of the forty chapters. I propose you consider taking a 40-day journey, using this book as a devotional, to digest and assimilate every verse more fully as it relates to your own personal walk with the Lord.

In Luke 9:23, Jesus said, "Whoever wants to be my disciple must deny themselves and take up their cross daily and follow me." James shares his journey of taking to heart these words of Jesus. Every disciple of Christ will experience a *crisis of belief* at various times; indeed, for our faith to be proven genuine it must be tried by fire and purified like gold.

After reading this autobiography, the one word I believe best describes James' faith journey is perseverance, which reminds me of the story in the Bible about the persistent widow. In this story, the widow's persistence proved her unrelenting faith. At the end of the story, Jesus states, "When the Son of Man comes, will He really find faith on the earth?" The challenge set before each of us is whether or not we will dare to walk down the path of genuine, proven faith that few follow.

Juliet Canha,
District Pastor, Forerunner Church

Foreword
To the First Edition
(Revised and Shortened)

God said: "I will live and walk among them.
I will be their God, and they will be my people.
Therefore, come out from among unbelievers, and separate
yourselves from them, says the LORD.
Don't touch their filthy things, and I will welcome you.
And I will be your Father, says the LORD Almighty."
~ 2 Corinthians 6:16–17 ~

I've known James for a long time, but it wasn't until I took a sales position with the same legal publishing company that I really began to get to know James. He was a great salesperson who was consumed with himself, winning awards, and making as much money as he could.

On April 5th, 2003, the Lord chose James to become a special witness to verify God's amazing grace and truth. Everything that defined his perception about himself was stripped away. I watched God leading James through many *crises of belief* experiences that crucified his flesh. Once James recognized Jesus as his Savior, he counted the cost. He put his hand to the plow and has never looked back.

James invited me to come to Austin, Texas, to do ministry with him. I had no idea what God had planned for me. Talk about an eye-opening action-packed trip! I witnessed the power of God move in so many different ways! I've read in the Bible many times and have heard people say that there's power in the name of Jesus. But, for the first time, I really understood what that meant. I will never ever forget that exact moment it dropped from my head to my heart. I will forever be grateful.

James is a forerunner for Christ and a trailblazer for our generation. Like King David, he is "a man after God's own heart." His authentic and transparent testimony, from serving the devil to serving Jesus, will keep you reading his book until the end. After reading this book, you will understand what Jesus meant when He said, "You will do the same works that I have done and even greater works" (John 14:12). You will never be the same and you will never want to go back to lukewarm Christianity.

We as a body of believers need to begin operating in what God called us to do. We are to take back what the enemy has stolen! If not now, when? If not you, who? We need to be the church, not play church!

The Bible is true. Signs, wonders, and miracles do follow you when you walk down "The Narrow Path that Few Follow." They will always point to Jesus and give glory to the Father. Do not disregard James' testimony just because you did not learn certain things in church. God is waking up His people. If you haven't encountered the real Jesus, pay very close attention to what God commissioned James to write. His example is what it looks like to walk in true obedience and faith!

I am so excited that you are reading this book. I highly recommend sharing it with your family, friends, co-workers, and neighbors. When you do, they will discover the power needed to transform their lives. If they are already Christian, they will be challenged in their faith and desire more!

Laura Berndt,
Friend & Former Co-Worker
Southwestern Publishing Company & Lexis Nexis

Introduction

May God give you more and more grace and peace
as you grow in your knowledge of God and Jesus our Lord.
By his divine power,
God has given us everything we need for living a godly life.
We have received all of this by coming to know him,
the one who called us to himself.
~ 2 Peter 1:2–4 ~

I spent the first forty years of my life trying to learn how to live according to the worldly principles that govern most people. I've spent the last fifteen plus years trying to unlearn everything that the world taught me because NOW I understand what Jesus meant when He said, "The gateway to the abundant life is very narrow, only a few ever find it" (Matthew 7:14). **Crisis of Belief** *is the story of my life.*

This book is nonfiction, an account of my spiritual journey which I hope will help inspire and teach you how to walk down the very narrow path that few find and fewer follow. My story has helped redefine what others think about themselves and how they see others. It has taught ordinary people how to enter into a deep and personal relationship with God and helped them heal, grow, and reproduce as ambassadors of reconciliation to a lost world.

I hope this story of my life will help you, too.

At one time people believed that the world was flat because they trusted what everyone else thought. Later, we learned that the world is round. Have you ever formed strong opinions about something or someone and discovered later that you were totally wrong? It's one thing to hear stories about God, but head knowledge is different from knowing Jesus intimately.

Crisis of Belief is the depiction of a journey from secularism to spiritual consciousness. A vivid characterization of the two positions that have helped me is a scene from the movie "The Matrix." In it, Neo, who has been searching for the truth, is presented with a decision. Before he could move forward, he had to decide to give up everything he had previously thought was true.

Morpheus says something like this;

> "Do you want to know what the truth is? The truth is, the matrix is everywhere. It is all around us. You can see it when you look out your window or when you turn on your television. You can feel it when you go to work, pay taxes, and when you go to church. It is the world that has been pulled over your eyes to blind you from the truth. The truth is that we are slaves who, like everyone else, were born into bondage, born into a prison that we can't smell or taste or touch. A prison for our minds. Unfortunately, no one can be told what the matrix is. You have to see it for yourself. You have to choose between the red pill and the blue pill."
>
> *[The Matrix, written by the Wachowski Brothers, produced by Village Roadshow Pictures, 1999].*

If you decide to travel with me on this journey, just like in the movie, you have to choose to swallow the red pill. In this case, it represents a willingness to open up your mind, pray about what you read, follow my suggestions, and seek God for wisdom and direction. You, too, have to be willing to give up what you believe about how the world operates.

If you like great adventures, this journey may be the most difficult challenge that you've ever faced. Sometimes, you'll feel like you've been thrown into a mixed martial arts fight with the reigning MMA heavyweight champion of this world. It doesn't take long to figure out that Satan is real and that he doesn't fight fair. The devil attacks our weaknesses in spiritual battlegrounds that have names like Past Mistakes, Mental Strongholds, and the Valley of Despair. Later, we finally learn that spiritual warfare turns out to be a blessing in disguise because a *crisis of belief* puts us into a unique position for God to teach us how to break free from all types of bondage; even the most horrific events that can scar many people for life.

But first, let me explain what I mean by a *crisis of belief*.

Two positions constantly pull at the soul of everyone who is actively seeking God's will. The spirit of antichrist, which often disguises itself as common sense, is guided by modern day false teachers. The media, politicians, and TV personalities are deceiving the masses through "secular humanism" teachings which latch onto self-centered thoughts and human reasoning. Its followers rely on their own strength, abilities, resources, connections, timing, and human efforts. The other position, which recognizes God's grace at work, steps into faith by partnering with Christ Jesus' Spirit who empowers us to overcome in the very real battle that takes place between two worlds—

will we obey the Lord of heaven and earth or will we obey the spirit of antichrist which attempts to control us through secular humanistic thoughts?

We face a *crisis of belief* when we have to choose between listening to God and listening to ourselves (or the enemy). Logic and common sense are not helpful in distinguishing between the two. The enemy's voice, which tries to get us to make quick decisions, sounds very reasonable and it entices us by telling us what our emotions want to hear. I've found that God's voice, which is a "knowing," stamps an indelible "thought impression" upon our soul. It's as if it rises up from inside of me, as if from my heart or from my spirit. If I am patient to wait, when I "hear" God's Spirit again, it confirms what I believe God spoke, and it resonates with holiness, peacefulness, truth, and love. (It never contradicts Scripture.) I recognize it and somehow just "know" it is God. So throughout this book when I refer to a spiritual knowing or thought impressions, this is what I am talking about. If you have to wonder if it is God, it probably is not.

God is always faithful, loving, kind, gentle, patient and considerate. He wants us to know His voice so He provides the grace that is sufficient to hear God through "thought impressions." When we ask the Holy Spirit for help, we express faith since faith is the substance of things hoped for. God speaks faith into existence, too, but we still need to do our part by stepping towards the direction we believe God is leading us, which sometimes requires making adjustments, so that we can align our will underneath God's grace which empowers us with supernaturally creative thoughts, divine appointments, invisible resources, and a childlike faith that feeds us through God's divine umbilical cord. Self-willpower eventually wears itself out because it is dependent upon human self-sufficiency. However, God's administration of grace enables all things to become possible for us. But first, we must step into the grace, through faith, which enables us to overcome our initial *crisis of belief.*

Since God desires for us to enter into a deep and personal relationship with Him, don't be afraid to ask God questions. Talk to him just like you would your best friend. Practice listening for Him to speak and expect Him to respond to answers that you seek. Since God speaks things into existence, a "knowing" or "thought impression" could be a word of wisdom that solves a very difficult situation, a preview of a futuristic event, an answer to prayer, or another component of God's grace displayed throughout the stories encapsulated throughout this book that document the multifaceted administration of God's supernatural grace.

During this journey, there are many forks in the road. God places red and blue pill-type choices in our pathway to help us to make better decisions by relying on His grace. While traveling down this narrow pathway which keeps getting narrower, the truth purifies our thoughts. Along the way, we are guided by an inner consciousness that leads those who are willing to be led. Like the biblical story about the road to Emmaus, this one comes with a surprise guest. When you awaken, you'll discover that Jesus has been with you all along and that finding this book wasn't an accident.

For more than fifteen years now I've been traveling down the narrow path that few follow. Everyone's equilibrium gets shaken from time to time because of bondage linking us to childhood wounds, the cares of this world, sin and carnal thoughts, and demonic attacks, all of which attempt to keep us from fulfilling our spiritual destinies. Although my journey has been filled with all kinds of signs, wonders, miracles, and blessings, at times I've questioned my own sanity, and at other times I've felt totally lost until I stepped into God's spoken grace which enabled me to overcome in a *crisis of belief*.

Will we trust God or will we trust ourselves?

The spiritual principles that are interwoven throughout my personal testimony apply to everyone's life, but each of our journeys is unique. I hope my testimony encourages you to pray about what it truly means to be a Christ follower. If you are traveling down the narrow path that few find and fewer follow, most people will think you are crazy since following Jesus is radically different from how the vast majority of people live their lives. God's grace is magnified when He takes a tragic life, full of many failures, and turns it around into a glorious victory which gives hope, inspiration, and guidance to others.

God often recruits people from the pit, rather than from the pedestal. Since my life was in crisis stage before I began following Christ, it was easier to quit my six-figure job to follow Him. In the beginning, while God was reconstructing my life, I lived off my savings account. When that money ran out, I felt led to cash in my stocks, IRAs, and 401(k). After I pushed all of my investments into the pot, I pursued God full-time. When that money ran out, I sold or gave away everything that I owned, including the contents of my homes, just for the privilege of following Christ.

The biggest *crisis of belief* challenge that I faced in my life was when God birthed a vision in me that targeted 360 churches in the Greater Austin community. Although I didn't know anything about music or festivals, God called me to put together two back-to-back Power of the Cross Festivals (2006 and 2007) in the heart of downtown Austin and to pay for it with my life savings. There wasn't any way for me to recoup my savings since God told me to make the festivals free. That *crisis of belief* was magnified even more since I didn't have a clue how to organize a three-stage music festival with twenty-seven bands. Although some very powerful religious leaders tried to stop the festivals from taking place, my team was faithful to what God called us to do which included giving away $55,000 worth of food through a relationship that I had with House of Faith in Wichita, Kansas.

Between the two festivals, God led me to become an executive television producer at a local television station. In spite of the fact that I didn't know anything about producing, editing, or directing, I became a producer of five weekly Christian TV shows which was a first as a volunteer for that TV station. Then once again, I ran out of money. That is when I sold the only thing I had left—the condo I had been living in—and bought an old RV and headed out West to go sightseeing until that money ran out.

I've moved thirteen times in fifteen years (2003–2018). Ten of those moves were provisional moves around the Greater Austin area. Three times God led me to relocate to other states where I didn't know anyone. It should have been impossible to live without a job that provided income, but when I did, I began to truly understand the magnitude of God's faithfulness.

In 2008, the Spirit led me to Springfield, Missouri, to help start a church that didn't plant. With fifty dollars left to my name, a divine appointment led to God replanting me in a low-income housing facility called the Franciscan Villa Apartments. I worked two graveyard shifts as a security officer in exchange for a room, three hot meals a day, and the basic necessities of life. While living there, I persevered through all kinds of crises of belief which led to me evangelizing, teaching Bible studies, discipling people, and conducting a funeral service. God Himself enabled me to bloom where He planted me.

In 2010, God orchestrated a series of *crisis of belief* situations which closed doors in Springfield and suddenly opened up new doors to take me back to Austin. A series of supernatural housing provisions led to multiple volunteer ministry opportunities and then God's Spirit led me back into sales, at which I failed miserably, to prove to me that I couldn't go back to my old life; my old life was crucified so that I could become a bondservant of Christ.

While God's Spirit was leading me down the narrow path that few find, I thought I knew where God was leading me, but then I began to realize I didn't have a clue. The frustrating part is trying to figure it out. The joy is in not knowing, learning to let go, trusting, and being surprised. For example, one day God led me to a stranger's house to pray for a young woman who had just been diagnosed by two different doctors as having cancer. Not only did God supernaturally heal her, but six months later the Lord led me and a ministry sister back to her house to document her healing. We also got to witness God heal one of her neighbors who was suffering from a women's blood issue.

God's administration of grace has enabled me to persevere in spite of huge challenges. Although very few people have ever recognized or sown anything into supporting my ministry, God's unusual provision has enabled me to serve full-time in ministry for over fifteen years. Recently, I discovered that I could cash in a pension fund that I didn't even know that I had. I opened the letter while facing a *crisis of belief* which this time was moving from Austin, Texas to Kansas City, Missouri, to serve as a volunteer under various IHOPKC ministries.

The chapters that follow document my personal testimony which include stories such as a burning-bush type experience that led to my conversion months after I turned 40. Jesus told me personally that my sins were forgiven. During my own personal walk to Emmaus, I literally stood before Christ's eyes. My physical life has been saved and my finances have been restored supernaturally several times. I've also witnessed Christ heal people miraculously.

I've served under churches and para-church ministries, participated in Kairos Prison Ministry and Bill Glass' Behind the Walls Ministry. I was ordained apostolically and then ordained others, led hundreds of people to Christ, written two books which thousands have read, and I spend exorbitant amounts of time and energy discipling people through my personal Facebook page.

I have been an eyewitness to many other signs, wonders, and miracles, but this book is limited to what the Holy Spirit has led me to write. I clearly understand why John said in his gospel that Jesus did many other things but it would be too difficult to record everything (John 21:25).

We are here on earth but for a twinkling of an eye, but our eternal rewards will last forever. Jesus said, "Look! I am coming soon, and my reward is with me to pay each one according to what they do!" (Revelation 22:12). For believers, the judgment seat of Christ isn't a place of punishment. It is a place where rewards will be given or lost depending on our willingness to align our lives with the kingdom principles described in the Bible that are exemplified throughout this book.

James Timothy Butt

Scripture References

Then the two from Emmaus told their story
of how Jesus had appeared to them
as they were walking along the road,
and how they had recognized him as he was breaking the bread.
(Luke 24:35)

But to all who believed him and accepted him,
he gave the right to become children of God.
(John 1:12)

"My thoughts are nothing like your thoughts," says the LORD.
"And my ways are far beyond anything you could imagine.
For just as the heavens are higher than the earth, so my ways are higher
than your ways and my thoughts higher than your thoughts."
(Isaiah 55:8–9)

The thief's purpose is to steal and kill and destroy.
My purpose is to give them a rich and satisfying life.
(John 10:10)

Becoming "Born Again"

Chapter 1

Is that All There Is?

The gateway to life is very narrow and the road is difficult,
and only a few ever find it.
~ Matthew 7:14 ~

When my first marriage failed, I was convinced that it was my ex-wife's fault. When my second marriage failed, I started to realize that something might be wrong with me. When I became single again, I dove deeper into my addictions to numb the emotional pain that was connected to childhood wounds. When the booze stopped working, I discovered crack, which pulled me down really hard, really quick. Until I hit rock-bottom, I didn't realize how lost I was. I had been listening to the voice in my head telling me that I could fix my problems without anyone's help. Suddenly, I found myself reaching for a life rope in the middle of the ocean during a hurricane. I finally had the desperation of a drowning man, but by then the ship had already capsized, and along with it, every area of my life was in ruins.
I was shipwrecked.

The American dream for many is a home, two cars, kids, and a white picket fence. If we reach these milestones, the focus shifts to raising the kids, helping the kids go to college, and saving money for retirement. What happens to us when we reach all our goals and still feel incomplete is usually called the midlife identity crisis.

I experienced that midlife crisis right before I turned 40. My second wife and I had $300,000 sitting in the bank, stock funds, and a nice retirement plan. I had a successful career, we lived the country-club lifestyle, we were able to travel to many great places all over the world, and we could buy most of the things that we wanted. Although it sounds great, I began to search for reasons to keep on living. I had it all but I was still empty. And I was still suffering from childhood wounds. We reached what many would describe as the pinnacle of our careers; however, I never fully enjoyed it, because I lived in fear. I worried about our mortgage payments, how to keep up our lifestyle, and other worldly concerns which created tremendous stress. The truth is, I was miserable, but I didn't understand why.

Everyone wrestles with problems, concerns, fears, differing opinions, and incorrect religious beliefs. *Crisis of Belief* is, I hope, a transparent story of a journey of self-discovery that will enable you to take things suppressed subconsciously and expose them to the healing power that can be found when we step into a deep, committed, and very personal relationship with Christ.

I hope that my spiritual journey can help you learn from my mistakes. We can't change what we did yesterday, but together we can take a new journey down a narrow path that few find and fewer follow which will change your eternal perspective about life.

As an example, preventative medicine beats the crisis that you would find yourself in if you woke up one day while on vacation in a third world country and suddenly discovered that you needed emergency heart surgery. Unfortunately, most of us wait too long before we leap into action because we buy into the lie that tells us that we don't need to fix something that isn't totally broken. I bought into that lie and many others, and I have documented them throughout this book.

I could have saved myself and others a lot of pain if I had paid greater attention to the various symptoms that are described in the chapters that follow. Exposure of these symptoms should help you to crystallize your thoughts. But before you dive too deeply into spiritual consciousness, some self-reflection is needed so that you can get in touch with what is really going on in your head.

For now, let me simply say that it's impossible to grasp what I have to share if you are close-minded. If your life is perfect, don't change a thing. If your life isn't perfect, then try something new by allowing me to be your tour guide down that narrow road that few find and even fewer dare follow.

Remember Jesus Himself said, *"The gateway to life is very narrow and the road is difficult, and only a few ever find it"* (Matthew 7:14).

Scripture References

For the light makes everything visible.
This is why it is said,
"Awake, O sleeper, rise up from the dead,
and Christ will give you light."
(Ephesians 5:14)

Anyone who listens to my teaching and follows it is wise,
like a person who builds a house on solid rock.
Though the rain comes in torrents and the floodwaters rise,
and the winds beat against that house,
it won't collapse because it is built on bedrock.
(Matthew 7:24–25)

And what do you benefit if you gain the whole world
but lose your own soul?
Is anything worth more than your soul?
(Matthew 16:26)

Next the devil took him to the peak of a very high mountain
and showed him all the kingdoms of the world and their glory.
"I will give it all to you," he said,
"if you will kneel down and worship me."
"Get out of here, Satan," Jesus told him. "For the Scriptures say,
'You must worship the LORD your God and serve only him.'"
(Matthew 4:8–10)

Self-Reflection Questions

Is there is more to life than chasing the American dream?

Am I in denial? In emotional pain? Feeling empty or incomplete?

Do I need to change my life?

What steps do I need to take?

Do I have an eternal perspective of life?

What does the Bible mean by "The gateway to life is very narrow and the road is difficult, and only a few ever find it"?

Meditate on the scripture verses in this chapter.
How do they apply to my life?

Chapter 2

A Wake-Up Call

And what do you benefit if you gain the whole world but lose your own soul?
Is anything worth more than your soul?
~ Matthew 16:26 ~

When I walked through the front door, Meredith was standing at the bar with her credit card in her hand, asking me what I wanted to drink. My willpower collapsed and I blurted out, "I'll have a Corona with lime," which turned out to be my first of many that night. The autopilot addiction urge came over me, and I left the bar so that I could drive to a place where I could score crack. I got into my car, drove from downtown Austin up I-35 and turned onto Highway 183 North. Suddenly, a sobering thought became crystal clear in my mind - not the kind of thought a man ordinarily thinks. The thought was, "What would God think about what I am about to do?" At that exact moment, a forty-foot tall cross lit up on my immediate right.

"Aha" moments are often misdiagnosed. Initially, they may take on the appearance of what some label a midlife crisis, but they are really spiritual growth opportunities dressed up in disguise. They grab our attention as if someone physically slapped us in the face. When I awoke, I suddenly found myself wrestling with new thoughts that were foreign to me up until that point. It was as if God reached into the deep dark pit to awaken me before I slipped into a permanent state of unconsciousness.

Circumstances and situations can be designed to grab our attention and even seem to scream at us. However, God also whispers to us through circumstances and situations. I was forty years old when God sent me a burning bush* in the shape of a forty-foot tall cross.

Many Americans live paycheck to paycheck. Few have emergency reserves. Many have accumulated huge debts and have maxed out their credit cards. Great paying jobs seem to be a thing of the past, pensions are underfunded, and retirement saving plans are being eliminated. On top of everything else, our world is changing at a breakneck speed and the political climate has created a tinderbox situation that could easily lead to the same kind of civil unrest which led to the Arab Spring movements that toppled foreign governments.

If you knew for sure that tragedy would bang on your front door, what kind of spiritual adjustments would you need to make now? The only true safety and security is a life built upon your relationship with Jesus Christ, the only rock-solid foundation that can withstand the troubling times ahead.

My foundation had cracks in it so it needed to be totally replaced. The next four chapters describe the background for that wake-up call that I received on State Highway 183.

The burning bush (experience) refers to the manifestation of the Spirit of God in the natural realm, with the purpose of getting our attention so that we are receptive to God's message. See Exodus 3:1-3.

Scripture References

God's law was given so that all people could see how sinful they were.
But as people sinned more and more,
God's wonderful grace became more abundant.
So just as sin ruled over all people and brought them to death,
now God's wonderful grace rules instead, giving us right standing with
God and resulting in eternal life through Jesus Christ our LORD.
(Romans 5:20–21)

These things happened to them as examples for us.
They were written down to warn us who live at the end of the age.
(1 Corinthians 10:11)

Do not remember the rebellious sins of my youth.
Remember me in the light of your unfailing love,
for you are merciful, O LORD.
The LORD. is good and does what is right;
he shows the proper path to those who go astray.
He leads the humble in doing right, teaching them his way.
The LORD. leads with unfailing love and faithfulness
to all who keep his covenant and obey his commands.
(Psalm 25:7–10)

Self-Reflection Questions

Am I spiritually awake? Am I conscious of God?

Is God trying to get my attention through circumstances or situations?

Do I have a relationship with the God who created me?

Do I need to be honest with myself, and make lifestyle changes now?

List everything that influences my mind, will, and emotions.

Meditate on the scripture verses in this chapter.
How do they apply to my life?

Chapter 3

Pain, Healing, & Forgiveness

Yes, I am the gate. Those who come in through me will be saved.
They will come and go freely and will find good pasture.
The thief's purpose is to steal and kill and destroy.
My purpose is to give them a rich and satisfying life.
~ John 10:9–10 ~

While growing up, my parents taught me right from wrong, and manners. Occasionally, our mother took my brother Ricky and me to St. James Lutheran Church, especially when we were younger. My father was raised a strict Catholic and wanted nothing to do with organized religion. We didn't own a Bible, let alone read one, and no one ever accused us of being Christians when we stepped outside the four walls of the church, but I believed that God might exist and I learned how to say the sinner's prayer. When I posted on Facebook that I had become a Christian, my childhood next-door neighbor posted, "If Jimmy Butt can become a Christian, anyone can."

Let's face it, life isn't easy. It's difficult being a child, raising a child, or handling the other pressures that come with being an adult. Very few of us were raised with a silver spoon in our mouths, and the ones that I've met, often seemed more messed up than the rest of us. To my parents' credit, they fed, clothed, cared for, and loved us the best way they knew how.

I try being compassionate towards others since we never know what others might have had to overcome. I can't imagine what it would have been like growing up in poverty, being molested, living with parents that did hardcore drugs, or having a mother who sold herself as a prostitute. I do know that my life proves beyond a shadow of a doubt that God can turn around any situation, regardless of how bad we've messed up or how far we've fallen.

My parents did the best they could, but they weren't perfect. My dad was an alcoholic and my mother also had a drinking problem. Although the alcoholic "gene" skipped over my brother, I became just like my parents. Oftentimes, alcoholics are emotionally immature, selfish, self-centered, verbally combative, and extremely narcissistic. Many suffer from anxiety issues and low self-esteem. It's hard to engage in real discussions with alcoholics because those who haven't experienced a spiritual awakening still see the world as through the lens of a movie director trying to rearrange everyone's behavior to fit into the alcoholic's narrative.

My parents didn't communicate very well with each other. They taught us that we weren't supposed to talk about our feelings, so we didn't. We tiptoed around our house to avoid conflict with my mother who got upset easily. My older brother and I were never very close growing up. He said it was my fault and I blamed him. It has taken many years, but after being filled with God's Spirit, I was able to walk in the humility needed to reconcile our relationship. Praise the Lord!

While growing up, my mother told me that I was just like her. I told myself many times that I would never grow up to be like my parents. But that is exactly what happened; I despised her until God changed us both. Once we both changed and after my first two marriages failed, I was able to see things from a different perspective during the latter years of her life.

My mother's doctor prescribed medicines that helped my mother overcome the anxiety issues that she struggled with most of her life. I loved talking to her over the phone during the last dozen years of her life. I rarely went home, then a door opened to take me back to New Jersey during the summer of 2013. While praying, the Lord revealed to me that my trip home would be the last time that I would see my mother alive, though she appeared to be in fairly good health.

When I went home, I told my mother what the Lord had revealed to me and then I asked her if I could pray for her. When I did, the Holy Spirit spoke powerfully through me in what seemed like a ten-minute prayer. I'll never forget the look on her face while I prayed. It was as if an angel touched her soul, restored her innocence, and taught her how to pray. Afterward, she became a person of prayer. She loved calling me to let me know that she was praying for me. She died suddenly, one year later.

My father's drinking got worse over the years but we continued to keep in touch by phone until he died unexpectedly following hip surgery. Right before he went into the hospital, we had a heart-to-heart phone conversation, and I encouraged him to get right with the Lord. I am told a priest went into his hospital room and had a private conversation with him before he was operated on. I have no idea if my father is or isn't with Christ right now, which is one of the reasons I am so passionate about sharing the Gospel with others before it is too late.

The last fifteen years of my father's life weren't pretty. When I asked my family if they wanted me to come home for his funeral, they told me not to bother because they didn't think anyone would show up.

When I was young, I just wanted to feel normal. I spent the first forty years of my life self-medicating in an attempt to wipe away stress and emotional pain. I tried booze, women, drugs, nice trips around the world, big houses, multiple marriages, success, and lots of other things, but nothing filled the emptiness that I felt inside. It wasn't until after I turned forty and hit rock bottom, in complete brokenness, that I discovered a personal relationship with Jesus Christ was the answer to every problem that I had and the fulfillment of some things which I didn't even know that I needed. It was through Him that I began to realize how much I had hurt others and that my life was exactly like the biblical story called the Parable of the Lost Son (see Luke 15:11–32). I would encourage you to read and pray about those verses.

Scripture References

Make allowance for each other's faults,
and forgive anyone who offends you.
Remember, the LORD forgave you, so you must forgive others.
(Colossians 3:13)

Direct your children onto the right path,
and when they are older, they will not leave it.
(Proverbs 22:6)

And don't address anyone here on earth as "Father",
for only God in heaven is your spiritual Father.
(Matthew 23:9)

My child, pay attention to what I say.
Listen carefully to my words.
Don't lose sight of them.
Let them penetrate deep into your heart,
for they bring life to those who find them,
and healing to their whole body.
(Proverbs 4:20–22)

"LORD, help!" they cried in their trouble,
and he saved them from their distress.
He sent out his word and healed them,
snatching them from the door of death.
(Psalm 107:19–20)

Watch out!
Don't let your hearts be dulled by carousing and drunkenness,
and by the worries of this life.
Don't let that day catch you unaware, like a trap.
For that day will come upon everyone living on the earth.
Keep alert at all times.
And pray that you might be strong enough to escape these coming horrors
and stand before the Son of Man.
(Luke 21:34–36)

Self-Reflection Questions

Do I have childhood emotional wounds?

Am I self-medicating in an attempt to ease my stress and emotional pain?

Am I willing to invite Jesus into my heart to heal my emotional wounds?

Do I believe that God is willing to help me overcome everything I am struggling with?

Is there someone who has hurt me whom I need to forgive?

Is there someone I have hurt whom I need to ask for forgiveness?

Meditate on the scripture verses in this chapter.
How do they apply to my life?

Chapter 4

My Failed Marriages

"For I hate divorce!" says the LORD, the God of Israel.
"To divorce your wife is to overwhelm her with cruelty,"
says the LORD of Heaven's Armies.
"So guard your heart; do not be unfaithful to your wife."
~ Malachi 2:16 ~

My first wife was a smart, beautiful, ambitious, hard-working woman who had good morals. After our careers took off, we built Melissa's two-story stucco dream home located down the street from Great Hills Country Club in Austin, Texas. I wish I could tell you that this story ended here and that we lived happily ever after. Unfortunately, our marriage didn't stand a chance since I didn't have a clue what it meant to live a Christ-centered life.

My life's motto was, "Work hard and party harder." With my career flourishing, I played a lot of golf. It didn't take long to find other young couples from the country club who loved to party as much as I did. This reminded me of the social gatherings my parents shared with their drinking buddies.

Melissa outgrew partying while I wanted to party even more. Blowing off steam is how I numbed the emotional insecurities of the wounded child within. Suddenly, Melissa stopped going to the county club and started putting her foot down when it came to my foolish drinking. There were other disagreements, too. From that point on, it seemed like we were always entangled in power struggles designed to get me to change. In my delusional mind, I can remember thinking that she tricked me into marrying her by pretending to be someone that she wasn't. What I didn't understand back then is that love is an action verb that requires effort, selflessness, and compromise. My brother was right—my marriages failed because I was a selfish, self-centered, and an emotionally immature little boy, which I learned later is common for alcoholics.

Melissa was a wonderful woman. It wasn't until many years later, after God led me into recovery, that I began to see things from a totally different perspective. Since the wounded child within needed divine healing, I was masking my issues through excessive drinking.

The divorce process was fairly simple. I gave Melissa the house, almost everything in it, the country club membership, and our two dogs. I kept our stocks, my 401(k), the IRAs, and my pension plan. After I moved from the house, I moved into an upscale apartment complex to be near people who took partying to a new level. When the masking effects of alcohol stopped working, I dove into drugs to numb the stress, emotional pain, and insecurities that targeted the wounded child within who was now also a divorcé. Besides booze, the typical weekend now included cocaine, pot, mushrooms, and chasing after single women at local night clubs in Austin.

I met my second wife, Terri, at a bar. She wasn't drinking at that time, because she said that she was trying to quit. My life was spiraling out of control, so instead of paying attention to that warning sign, I thought we might be good influences on each other. We dated for a short time, got married too quickly, and bought a home at Berry Creek Country Club, in Georgetown, Texas. I was back to playing golf and still making six figures. It didn't take long to find other young couples from the country club who loved to drink as much as we did.

Yes, as silly as this broken record sounds, insanity is doing the same thing over and over again and expecting different results. The main difference this time was I had a partying buddy who liked to drink as much as I did and she started pulling in major money in her newly launched real estate career.

At the height of our marriage, we had $300,000 sitting in the bank, stocks, and IRAs, and we took exotic vacations overseas. Underneath the surface, we both had a lot of issues that we were dealing with individually and as a couple. Looking back now, our lives were similar to the theme in the movie *Groundhog Day*. Our record kept skipping between work hard, play harder, repeat past mistakes, and do far more stupid things.

Terri and I finally reached the point where neither of us wanted to be married to each other, so I moved out. The divorce process was fairly simple. I gave her the house, everything in it, the country club membership, and our two cats. I kept our stocks, my 401(k), IRAs, and my pension plan. Sound familiar? My first failed marriage was costly. The second divorce, on top of everything else, set me back even more.

Does this sound like life on the right track?

Scripture References

Give honor to marriage,
and remain faithful to one another in marriage.
God will surely judge people who are immoral
and those who commit adultery.
(Hebrews 13:4)

And do not bring sorrow to
God's Holy Spirit by the way you live.
Remember, he has identified you as his own,
guaranteeing that you will be saved on the day of redemption.
Get rid of all bitterness, rage, anger, harsh words,
and slander, as well as all types of evil behavior.
Instead, be kind to each other,
tenderhearted, forgiving one another,
just as God through Christ has forgiven you.
(Ephesians 4:30–32)

Now repent of your sins and turn to God,
so that your sins may be wiped away.
(Acts 3:19)

But if we confess our sins to him,
he is faithful and just to forgive us our sins
and to cleanse us from all wickedness.
(1 John 1:9)

Self-Reflection Questions

What are the relationship 'failures' I am struggling with?
Friendships? Family? Marriage?

Am I doing the same thing over and over again and expecting different results?

Do I drink too much?

Is it time to get help for troubling addictions?

What adjustment do I need to make to live a Christ-centered lifestyle?

Meditate on the scripture verses in this chapter.
How do they apply to my life?

Chapter 5

A Checkup from the Neck Up

For all that is secret will eventually be brought into the open,
and everything that is concealed will be brought to light
and made known to all.
~ Luke 8:17 ~

The six months following my second divorce I was completely out of control. Somehow, I still kept my job, but I found myself spending three to five days a week playing with all kinds of toys that you would only find in the devil's sandbox. It's one thing to have blackouts from drinking, say stupid things after snorting cocaine, or hallucinate after eating mushrooms, but smoking crack elevated my binge drinking and drug use to a whole different level of insane foolishness.

In crackhead circles, everyone is either a buyer, a dealer, a freeloader, or a dope prostitute (someone who sells their body to feed their addictions). When I entered into this circle, it didn't take long to find addicts to teach me where to buy drugs, how to smoke, which hotels were party friendly, and where to find others who were just as lost as I was, looking for someone to get high with.

The first time I smoked crack, I thought it would be a one-time thing. Months went by before I tried it again. After doing it a few more times, weeks separated the times in between. Before long, whenever I drank, I found myself smoking crack. I tried limiting my drinking but that didn't help. I stopped drinking, but much to my surprise, I couldn't stop the overwhelming desire to feed my crack addiction.

If we did a complete and thorough evaluation of your life, what would we learn? If we interviewed your family, friends, co-workers, and doctor, would we find that you are confronting life problems, circumstances, and situations or would we find that you are masking pain with alcohol, drugs, sex, religion, overeating, materialism, or work? If we dug deeper and hired a private detective, would we discover deep secrets which you've kept hidden from everyone including the people who matter most in your life? If God intervened by peeling back the cover of your soul, would we find that you live a Christ-centered, faith-based life or that you are running out of options because you are barely holding on? I was guilty of all the above.

If a team of mental health specialists ran tests and took x-rays of your brain, what would they discover? How do you cope when sudden tragedies strike without warning or when life throws you a curve ball? If our team of experts took a CT scan image of your brain, would the cross-sections reveal a life worth living or layers of troubling thoughts? If we did a sleep study, would the test indicate that you sleep peacefully or that you toss and turn throughout the night because you live in constant fear of hidden areas of your life finally being exposed? My guilt became unbearable.

If we brought together a psychologist, a sociologist, and a behavior therapy specialist, what would we learn about your mental health and well-being? Did you know that the list of famous people who have taken their own lives is so long that Wikipedia has to break it down by alphabetical order? Have you had any suicidal thoughts? Are you constantly trying to put out forest fires because you are living life on the edge of self-destruction? I am asking these pointed questions because of what I've personally experienced.

If you died tomorrow, would you spend eternity with God or would you be eternally separated from God and those you love? Are you sure? Would anyone really care? What would people say about you at your funeral? How many people do you think would even bother to attend? What would be the final words written on your gravestone? These questions might seem strange but my father's sudden death and countless other things have caused me to get my own affairs in order and look at life from the eternal perspective.

Crisis of belief moments are fertile ground—opportunities when faith can be cultivated. What sometimes appears horrific ends up lightening our loads because it sets us free from the burdens that we carry on our shoulders and the nightmares that make it hard to get a good night's sleep. My personal testimony includes stories that incorporate coping mechanisms, escapism, blaming others, denial, false idols, religious traps, and playing with dangerous toys in the devil's sandbox.

When we choose denial, at some point our problems resurface. When they do, we find ourselves having to deal with the same problems that have grown bigger. Escapism can numb the pain temporarily, but eventually, everything hidden finds its way back up to the surface. When it does, compounding interest affects innocent victims who become casualties of spiritual warfare. I know how dangerous it is to ignore the warning signs because untreated issues eventually lead into a bottomless pit.

Scripture References

But the Lord said to Samuel,
"Don't judge by his appearance or height,
for I have rejected him.
The Lord doesn't see things the way you see them.
People judge by outward appearance,
but the Lord looks at the heart."
(1 Samuel 16:7)

Be honest in your evaluation of yourselves,
measuring yourselves by the faith God has given us.
(Romans 12:3)

Make allowance for each other's faults,
and forgive anyone who offends you.
Remember, the Lord forgave you,
so you must forgive others.
(Colossians 3:13)

Then Jesus said, "Come to me, all of your who are weary
and carry heavy burdens, and I will give you rest.
Take my yoke upon you.
Let me teach you, because I am humble and gentle at heart,
and you will find rest for your souls.
For my yoke is easy to bear,
and the burden I give you is light."
(Matthew 11:28–30)

Self-Reflection Questions

What is the state of my mental health and spiritual well-being?

Do I have suicidal thoughts? Do I understand that those thoughts are not my own but are actually suggestions that come from the devil?

Am I constantly trying to put out forest fires because I am living life on the edge of self-destruction?

Am I confronting life problems, circumstances, and situations effectively?

Am I masking pain with alcohol, drugs, sex, religion, overeating, materialism, or work?

Do I have secrets which need to be brought out into the open and shared?

If I died tomorrow, would I spend eternity with God, or be eternally separated from those whom I love?

Chapter 6

Playing in the Devil's Playground

As a dog returns to its vomit, so a fool repeats his foolishness.
~ Proverbs 26:11 ~

Initially, I limited my partying to weekend nights. Before long, it was common for me to stay up three days without sleep. When I thought things started getting out of hand, I drew an imaginary line in the sand. I swore to myself that I would never allow myself to hit the crack pipe after midnight on Saturday nights. Three months later I blew through yet another promise when I stayed up for six days straight with barely a few hours of sleep.

I had morals before I started free falling into the demonic realm. The devil picked apart my morals, one by one, through a series of compromising choices until one day I woke up and discovered that I was morally bankrupt. When I started down this path, I had self-respect but by now that was all gone and I didn't have a clue how to get it back. One thing led to another and then, during a brief moment of clarity, I realized that I signed over the rights to my free-will. It was then that I realized that Satan had deleted the word "free" and taken total possession of my will! The devil had attached a ball to the chains that were firmly linked around my childhood wounds and divorce failures. It became harder to live with myself because my guilt had become unbearable.

The devil's trickery painted me into a mental corner. My mind became a prison. My new surroundings became a dark dungeon. The walls were thick. My thoughts were cloudy. I tried to collect my thoughts in smoke-filled crack rooms, which made it more difficult to think. I wanted to die. I finally crossed the threshold into a permanent state of hopelessness. My death certificate was dated and signed after I took my last crack-pipe hit on April 4th, 2003. I don't need to try and imagine what Hell might be like. I found it on my own through childhood wounds, alcoholism, the pride of life, the lust of the flesh, failed marriages, and crack addiction. I didn't see the fire, but God did show me the ugliness of my sinful nature. I couldn't even look at myself in the mirror.

It took incredible mercy to save me from my own stupidity. It was not some kind of religious effort initiated by me that pulled me out of the muck by my own bootstraps. I know for a fact that God reached into the gates of Hell, grabbed me from Satan's grip, and recruited me for a special calling which included writing this book, *Crisis of Belief.*

Scripture References

This is a trustworthy saying, and everyone should accept it:
Christ Jesus came into the world to save sinners-
and I am the worst of them all.
But God had mercy on me so that Christ Jesus
could use me as a prime example of
his great patience with even the worst sinners.
Then others will realize that they,
too, can believe in him and receive eternal life.
(1 Timothy 1:15–16)

God's law was given so that all people could see how sinful they were.
But as people sinned more and more,
God's wonderful grace became more abundant.
So just as sin ruled over all people and brought them to death,
now God's wonderful grace rules instead,
giving us right standing with God
and resulting in eternal life through Jesus Christ our LORD.
(Romans 5:20–21)

So humble yourselves before God.
Resist the devil,
and he will flee from you.
(James 4:7)

Self-Reflection Questions

Am I making compromising moral choices that destroy my self-worth?

Can I face staring at myself in the mirror, or is my guilt too unbearable?

Have I sold my soul to Satan? Do I want it back?

Meditate on the scripture verses in this chapter.
How do they apply to my life?

Chapter 7

Becoming God-Conscious

*And God confirmed the message by giving signs and wonders and
various miracles and gifts of the Holy Spirit whenever he chose.*
~ Hebrews 4:2 ~

*By the age of 40, the devil had a firm grip on my mind, will, and emotions.
But God worked through people like a partying buddy of mine who invited me
to a "Red" themed social party in an exclusive part of West Austin. At that time,
I didn't recognize the prophetic significance of the color red or the number 40
found throughout the Bible. After I became aware of God, I began learning
how to connect spiritual dots like the ones sprinkled throughout these remaining
chapters.*

On Saturday night, a friend promised me three times that he would meet
me at the Red party at 9 p.m. sharp. He showed up two hours late. In the
meantime, I felt very uncomfortable being at a party where I didn't know
anyone, so I picked up my pace of chugging beers. Then I came across Carol,
whom I had dated a few times in between my first two divorces. She introduced me to her friend Todd M., who was standing next to her. Todd and I
would become friends. I didn't know it then, but it was God who connected
me to Todd who became instrumental in helping me turn my life around.
After we exchanged phone numbers, I left the party so that I could snort
cocaine with my friend who had finally shown up.

Todd invited me to go with him to one of my favorite night clubs a week
later. Like a slow-motion video being replayed, I can still remember standing
at the bar ordering a drink with my credit card in hand while looking back
at Todd asking him what he wanted to drink. He ordered a Coke. That was
when I learned that he didn't drink, nor had he been drinking at the Red party.
Then he informed me that both he and Carol were in recovery. Half-jokingly
I asked, "What? You go to AA?" When he said he did, I told him that I had
been exposed to recovery meetings after my arrest for DUI. Then I broke
down and admitted I needed help.

He said, "If you're serious, I can help you." I asked him a lot of questions, and by the end of the night, I decided to give recovery another shot, even though I could not imagine *not* drinking since a drinking lifestyle was all I had known my entire life. Todd took me to meetings every day that first week.

During one of those meetings, I heard an old man named Charles say, "If your life is perfect, don't change a thing. Just keep doing what you are already doing. If your life isn't perfect, try what was suggested to me in a room just like this one over twenty-seven years ago. Get down on your knees for thirty days in a row and ask God to come into your life, to help you and keep you sober, one day at a time. If you'll do that, your life will change dramatically." That struck a chord with me but not enough to get me to give it a try, since I was already motivated to turn my life around using my own willpower.

On Saturday I participated in a golf scramble tournament. Afterward, when my team hit the 19th green to drink, I had a Coke. Later, while driving home, my cell phone rang. It was Meredith, who convinced me to meet her and another friend at a bar on 8th Street. I went because I figured I could still have fun and just drink Coke.

When I walked through the front door, Meredith was standing at the bar with her credit card in her hand. Just like that night with Carol and Todd, I have an indelible memory of her standing at the bar with her credit card in hand, asking me what I wanted to drink. Unlike Todd, my willpower collapsed. In a weak moment I blurted out, "I'll have a Corona with lime," which turned out to be my first of many that night.

When the autopilot addiction urge came over me, I left the bar so that I could drive to a place where I could score crack. After I got into my car, I drove from downtown Austin, up I-35, and turned onto Highway 183 North. Suddenly, a sobering thought became crystal clear in my mind. That thought was not the kind of thought a lost sinful man thinks. The thought was, "What would God think about what I am planning to do?" At that exact moment, a forty-foot tall cross lit up on my immediate right.

It wasn't a physical burning bush, but in the spirit realm, it clearly represented a *burning bush* type of experience. Other things about that night proved to have profound significance as well.

Although I had driven down that highway thousands of times, I had never noticed the "Gethsemane" Lutheran Church, where the cross had suddenly appeared. (Gethsemane means garden of decision). Many identify it as the beautiful "stained" glass church (which represented my sinful condition) on Highway 183 between Lamar and Interstate 35 (Highway of Holiness). The church was constructed in 1962, which is the year I was born. I also learned later that the Pitman, New Jersey, Lutheran Church that I attended growing up is called St. "James" Lutheran Church.

What happened on April 2nd, 2003, was just like a private world-premiere preview from the movie *Bruce Almighty*, which was released to the public on May 23rd of that year. In the movie, before he made a conscious connection with God, Bruce said, "God, just give me a sign." As soon as Bruce said that, a truck pulled in front of him and signs started flashing before his very eyes.

Although I wasn't absolutely positive back then, I believed for a few seconds anyway, that God had just spoken to me. Then my self-centered thoughts shifted back to my quest to score dope. I can still remember thinking during those moments, "Forget God." After I made that conscious decision to turn my back on God, I called my dope connection to let them know I was on my way.

What makes this journey extremely difficult is the eighteen inches that separate a person's brain from experiencing God in their hearts. The heart is the wellspring of life. Upbringing, intellectual thoughts, worldly conditioning, spiritual mindsets, and other mental blocks are all obstacles to becoming God conscious, that is, experiencing God in our hearts.

One of the greatest gifts God gave humanity is the human brain. It is so fantastic that many books have been written about it and no book has even been written or read without its use. It empowers us to think, understand, learn, remember, judge, problem solve, and make decisions. There are hundreds of thinking styles, methods of thinking, and types of thoughts which include reasoning, abstract thinking, beliefs, common sense, critical thinking, decision-making, emotions, ideas, logic, personal experience, consciousness, sub-consciousness; just to name a few. Did you notice beliefs squeezed in between so many different kinds of thoughts?

Gandhi, Darwin, Hitler, Einstein, and hundreds of other influential thinkers used their brains to shape, mold, change, define, and redefine our conceptual thoughts about the world in which we live. Some led humanity in the right direction and others have caused great harm. Hitler and those following him killed six million Jews during the Holocaust. Jim Jones, who was the cult leader of the People's Temple in Jonestown, led more than 900 followers (including 300 children) to commit suicide by swallowing cyanide.

If we researched the historical formation of the world's religions, we would find that almost all of them were created for political reasons, identity purposes, control, manipulation, and/or for the sustainability of cultures. Buddha, Mohammed, the Dalai Lama, Joseph Smith, and hundreds of other influential religious thinkers impregnated, shaped, molded, changed, defined, or redefined variations of religious teachings. Have you ever heard of Anton LaVey? He was the founder of the Church of Satan as well as the author of *The Satanic Bible*. Jesus Himself made the statement that He is God incarnate. The others claimed to have received some special type of prophetic enlightenment from an angel.

There are over seven billion people in the world. The vast majority believe in some kind of conceptual understanding of a deity, which is why so many worship false idols. Then there are the agnostics who aren't sure what they believe. On the flip side, some subscribe to the Big Bang theory or Darwin's theory of evolution which really means that they believe that humanity is an accident. Then there are the atheists who are very strong believers. They are convinced that God doesn't exist!

Have you noticed a pattern throughout these first few chapters? As I said earlier, what makes this journey extremely difficult is the eighteen inches that separate a person's brain from his heart. Jesus said, "We must be born again" (John 3:3).

Scripture References

Samuel did not yet know the LORD because he had never had a message
from the LORD before. So the LORD called a third time, and once more
Samuel got up and went to Eli. "Here I am. Did you call me?"
Then Eli realized it was the LORD who was calling the boy.
So he said to Samuel, "Go and lie down again, and if someone calls again, say,
'Speak, LORD, your servant is listening.'" So Samuel went back to bed.
(1 Samuel 3:7–9)

One day when Moses was forty years old,
he decided to visit his relatives, the people of God.
(Acts 7:23)

And a great road will go through that once deserted land.
It will be named the Highway of Holiness.
(Isaiah 35:8)

"Come now, let's settle this," says the LORD. "Though your sins are like scarlet,
I will make them as white as snow. Though they are red like crimson,
I will make them as white as wool.
(Isaiah 1:18)

Then Moses raised his hand over the Red Sea,
and the LORD opened up a path through the water with a strong east wind.
(Exodus 14:21)

Then Jesus went with them to the olive grove called Gethsemane,
and he said, "Sit here while I go over there to pray."
(Matthew 26:36)

When we were utterly helpless,
Christ came at just the right time and died for us sinners.
(Romans 5:6)

With all my heart I will praise you, O LORD my God.
I will give glory to your name forever, for your love for me is very great.
You have rescued me from the depths of death.
(Psalm 86:12–13)

Self-Reflection Questions

What is standing in the way of experiencing God in my heart?

What are the thought patterns, mindsets, and mental blocks that are keeping me from becoming God conscious?

Am I aware of someone whom God has sent to help me turn my life around?

If Jesus was standing next to me, what would He say about my behavior?

Meditate on the scripture verses in this chapter.
How do they apply to my life?

Chapter 8

A New Life

This means that anyone who belongs to Christ has become a new person.
The old life is gone; a new life has begun!
~ 2 Corinthians 5:17 ~

I was up for three straight days partying before I finally fell asleep. After I woke up, I checked my phone. I noticed that Todd called a few times. He knew that I had fallen off the wagon since I disappeared for three days. His last message was, "Call me when you wake up." After I called Todd, he asked, "Are you ready to go to a meeting today?" I told him that I felt horrible, so the last thing I wanted to do was to go to a recovery meeting. He said, "That's the best time to go. I'll come by to pick you up."

When he hung up, I wanted to call him back to cancel but I didn't. I couldn't stop thinking about the brightly lit cross from three nights before. I wondered if God really did speak to me, and if he did, I wondered if he would give me another chance.

The recovery meeting began the normal way all meetings begin, and then they opened it up for discussion on that day's topic. Suddenly, the old man repeated exactly what I heard him say the previous week.

Charles said, "If your life is perfect, don't change a thing. Just keep doing what you are already doing. If your life isn't perfect, try what was suggested to me in a room just like this one over twenty-seven years ago. Get down on your knees for thirty days in a row and ask God to come into your life, to help you and keep you sober, one day at a time. If you'll do that, your life will change dramatically."

Before Charles even finished my heart nearly leaped out of my body. This time I couldn't wait to get home and follow the same exact instructions that had first caught my attention a week earlier. When Todd dropped me off at my apartment on April 5th, 2003, I got down on my hands and knees and cried out to God in complete humility and total brokenness. To the best of my recollection, I prayed this exact prayer:

"God, I don't know for sure if You are real, but if you are real, I am going to give

You a chance to prove it. For the next thirty days, I am going to get down on my hands and knees and give You a chance to prove to me that You are real. I am going to cry out to You as I've never cried out to You before. If You don't answer me or show me that You are real, I will never come to you again. I need help. Scratch that. I need a lot of help. I have a drinking problem. No, I am an alcoholic, and I am hooked on crack. I can't beat this on my own. I've tried and tried and tried. I know for sure that I can't beat this on my own. I need Your help. I need You to deliver me from alcoholism and crack addiction. And Jesus, if You are real, I need You to forgive me for all my sins. If You will help me, I'll do whatever you ask."

I was crying harder than I had ever cried in my whole life. As I got up off my knees, I noticed that my shirt was soaking wet and that a heavy weight seemed to have lifted off my shoulders. A very noticeable change had taken place.

New thoughts suddenly became crystal clear. The first thought was that there might just be a way out of my hopeless situation after all. I can remember thinking, if God is real and if He really did speak to me with that bright cross, then maybe He could do for me what I couldn't do for myself. Perhaps God does have the power to keep me sober. Perhaps God can help me find a way to get my life back on track. Still, I was lost, confused, and my shame was unbearable.

So I made a decision to ask Jesus to live in my heart at that very moment; April 5th, 2003. That decision broke loose the devil's claim to my life. God took a piece of His own Spirit and placed it into my soul, which pushed out darkness by flooding my soul with light. Suddenly, all things became possible again. I was able to look at myself in the mirror because the guilt and shame were removed when I became a *new creation* in Christ Jesus.

I didn't have to go to an inpatient or an outpatient treatment center. God performed a miracle when He delivered me from crack addiction and the desire to get drunk. For thirty days straight, I got down on my hands and knees and cried out for God, who delivered me from destructive thoughts, emotional pain, work stress, and my struggle to maintain sobriety! During the course of the next year, Todd helped teach me how to still have fun while changing my lifestyle choices. I celebrated sixteen years of sobriety on April 5th, 2019. Praise the Lord!

My past mistakes are just that. They are indefensible. I can't change yesterday. I could and did seek forgiveness from the people that I hurt, which was an important part of my recovery. I made amends when doing so didn't cause more harm. I've also learned how to forgive myself while following Christ down the narrow path that few follow.

What about you?

Scripture References

Trust in the Lord with all your heart;
do not depend on your own understanding.
(Proverbs 3:5)

Don't copy the behavior and customs of this world,
but let God transform you into a new person
by changing the way you think.
Then you will learn to know God's will for you,
which is good and pleasing and perfect.
(Romans 12:2)

But people who aren't spiritual
can't receive these truths from God's Spirit.
It all sounds foolish to them and they can't understand it,
for only those whohave been given God's Spirit
can understand what the Spirit means.
(1 Corinthians 2:14)

Jesus replied,
"I tell you the truth, unless you are born again,
you cannot see the Kingdom of God."
(John 3:3)

So humble yourselves before God.
Resist the devil,
and he will flee from you.
(James 4:7)

Self-Reflection Questions

Will I come to Jesus in total humility and brokenness?

In what ways can I humble myself?

Will I give God a chance to make all things right?

Will I let go of my old life and embrace a completely new life?

Will I let go of all my past mistakes, and hit the reset button?
List a specific mistake that you know you need to let go of.

Will I seek a deep and very personal relationship with Jesus?

What can I do to deepen my relationship with Jesus?

Chapter 9

Learning to Hear God's Voice

When I think of all this, I fall to my knees and pray to the Father,
the Creator of everything in heaven and on earth. I pray that from his glorious,
unlimited resources he will empower you with inner strength through his Spirit.
Then Christ will make his home in your hearts as you trust in him.
Your roots will grow down into God's love and keep you strong.
And may you have the power to understand, as all God's people should,
how wide, how long, how high, and how deep his love is.
May you experience the love of Christ, though it is too great to understand fully.
Then you will be made complete with all the fullness of life
and power that comes from God.
~ Ephesians 3:14–19 ~

God fed me spiritual milk until I became strong enough to walk. My good friend and co-worker Laura Berndt, months before I was saved, bought me a leather Bible with James Timothy Butt engraved on the cover and gave me a copy of Henry Blackaby's Experiencing God *workbook. It wasn't until after I was saved that I recognized the spiritual significance of her two gifts. God insured that I had the tools I needed to learn to recognize His voice and make sure that it was His that I was following rather than the voice of another.*

Experiencing God by Henry Blackaby was especially helpful because it helped me figure out how to adjust my life to God's will during *crisis of belief* situations divinely orchestrated by God—oftentimes initially revealed to me through no more than internal knowings.

When I first began reading the Bible, it was like trying to learn a foreign language, so God's Spirit led me to go to a Christian bookstore to buy a Bible study guide. While checking out, the cashier placed a free copy of a Christian worship compilation CD into my bag called *Go Out with Joy*.

At first, I hated listening to it because it was so different from the secular music I had listened to up until then. After playing the CD a few more times, I stopped listening to secular music since Christian music modeled the new life that God's Spirit was leading me to embrace.

Christian praise and worship music is extremely powerful. Through listening to worship music, I learned how to pray perfect intercessory prayers since most worship and praise music aligns with Scripture. God inhabits our thoughts when we praise Him. I also noticed that tormenting thoughts, including fear and depression, disappeared whenever I listened to worship music.

Here is another example of how God began teaching me to recognize and follow His voice. One day, another friend emailed me the daily portion of *Today God Is First* (TGIF) devotional by Os Hillman. While reading it, God spoke directly to me. What I mean by that is, I was arrested by an awareness of the presence of the One who first spoke to me during my initial *crisis of belief*. I felt God imparting understanding to me that could only have come from Him. A specific truth which applied to my life at that moment became real to me in a way my mind could never have thought up.

A week later, she emailed me another in the series. While reading it, I noticed God spoke directly to me for a second straight time, so this time I signed up to receive the free daily devotional myself. God used it as a spiritual tool to teach me deeper lessons about walking with Him.

What's important to know is that God wants to speak to us so we need to learn how to hear Him. Some of the more common communication channels He uses are scriptures, worship music, people, circumstances, situations, writings by godly people, dreams, visions, and internal knowings, such as I described above. Signs, wonders, and miracles suddenly became frequent events in my life.

Healing the wounded child within became a process of connecting the spiritual dots, which were also like bread crumbs that guided my path reassuring me that God was actively involved in every area of my life, including my struggle to recapture a life worth living.

I have learned over the years that there are two positions which constantly pull at the soul of someone who is actively seeking God; *self-will and God's will*. Guided by self-willpower, common sense latches onto what it believes is right. It relies on its own strength, abilities, resources, connections, judgments, timing, and efforts. The other position, which is God's will, aligns itself under the covering of humility, brokenness, obedience, and submission. It relies on supernaturally creative thoughts, divine appointments, invisible resources, and childlike faith that feeds us intravenously through God's divine umbilical cord.

Self-willpower eventually wears itself out because it is dependent upon self-sufficiency. However, God's will enables all things to become possible and is backed by the same power source that created the earth, heaven, solar systems, and galaxies. I have also learned that it takes time and patience to figure out the various nuances of Christianity, because there are all kinds of different religious church doctrines which act like bones to hold Christ's Church together. The challenge, while traveling down the narrow path that few find, is learning the difference between the various church doctrines, sorting through man-made traditions, listening to the Holy Spirit, and then applying the right context to each interpretation of Scripture.

Learning how to become a Christ follower is different from simply going to church or following theologians' teachings on Christianity. Learning to hear God's voice became the single most important factor in my life. His voice is often confirmed for me through circumstances or divine appointments.

One morning, on April 12th, 2003, while driving my SUV down Palmer Lane, I realized that I had been sober for a whole week. While driving, I started praising God for keeping me sober. Suddenly, I realized that I was at a red light located directly in front of the Austin nightclub where I had scored dope the week before. From the elevated vantage point of my SUV, I glanced down to my left and noticed a young man snorting cocaine in the car next to me.

Then God spoke to me. It wasn't an audible voice. It was very similar to the way God was teaching me to hear Him while reading the devotionals—conscious impressions in my thoughts which God had begun teaching me to recognize as Him. The Lord seemed to say, "This was you a week earlier. This man is lost in his sin. You can go back to this lifestyle or you can follow Me and do what I say. The choice is yours to make."

The next day I asked God to be Lord over every area of my life and not just a someday savior. Like it was yesterday, I can still remember praying, "God, I now know that You are real because I can see that You are working in every area of my life." I also asked God to allow me to live by faith and I thanked Him for giving me the miracle gift of sobriety.

I've thought about those prayers and the beginning steps of my faith journey many times over the last sixteen years. Little did I know back then that my desperate prayers for help would lead me to become a completely sold out, all in, radical follower of Jesus Christ. I call it crazy faith. If you are traveling down the narrow path that few find and fewer follow, most people will think you are crazy since following Jesus is radically different from how the vast majority of people live their lives.

Did you try to buy a "someday" eternal insurance policy by saying a few magic sinner-prayer words or have you reached out to Christ Jesus with an open and sincere heart?

Scripture References

And it is impossible to please God without faith.
Anyone who wants to come to him must believe that God exists and that
he rewards those who sincerely seek him.
(Hebrews 11:6)

Then he said, "I tell you the truth,
unless you turn from your sins and become like little children,
you will never get into the Kingdom of Heaven."
(Matthew 18:3)

Like newborn babies, you must crave pure spiritual milk
so that you will grow into a full experience of salvation.
Cry out for this nourishment, now that you
have had a taste of the Lord's kindness.
(1 Peter 2:2–3)

And having chosen them, he called them to come to him.
And having called them,
he gave them right standing with himself.
And having given them right standing, he gave them his glory.
(Romans 8:30)

Enter his gates with thanksgiving;
go into his courts with praise.
Give thanks to him and praise his name.
For the Lord is good.
His unfailing love continues forever,
and his faithfulness continues to each generation.
(Psalm 100:4–5)

All Scripture is inspired by God and is useful to teach us what is true
and to make us realize what is wrong in our lives.
It corrects us when we are wrong and teaches us to do what is right.
God uses it to prepare and equip his people to do every good work.
(2 Timothy 3:16–17)

Self-Reflection Questions

God desires to speak to me. Am I listening?

Do I hear his voice?

What are the ways that God can speak to me?

How can I learn to hear Him better?

Am I currently receiving inner strength through God's Spirit?

Am I guided by self-will marked by fear and insecurity, or am I guided by God's will and the Holy Spirit marked by perfect peace?

Which will I choose?

The Seed Planted in Good Soil

Chapter 10

The Narrow Path that Few Find

You can enter God's Kingdom only through the narrow gate.
The highway to hell is broad,
and its gate is wide for the many who choose that way.
But small is the gate and narrow the way that leads to life,
and only a few find it.
~ Matthew 7:13–14 ~

There is an invisible pathway interwoven throughout the Bible which has been hidden from the casual reader. The Old Testament refers to it as the Way of Holiness. The New Testament calls it the narrow path that very few find. Although there are clues throughout the Bible as to the pathway's existence, the revelatory meaning of its complete definition has been hidden from the self-righteous, prideful, egotistical, self-centered, and uncircumcised in heart.

Blessed are the poor, meek, humble, merciful, peacemakers, and those who mourn because they are positioned spiritually to tap into the supernatural grace that breaks through the bondage of mental strongholds, intellectual arguments, deeply entrenched thought processes, and human conditioning. Often referred to as common sense, these can be counterproductive to understanding God's ways which are actually perfectly designed to redefine our entire concept of reality.

At the beginning of this faith journey, mental thoughts can become barriers that block God's way. God allows those who submit themselves under His wisdom in humility, brokenness, and a yearning for more to find the invisible entrance to this spiritual journey of self-discovery that crushes captivity mindsets.

There is only one method required to learn what is the way, the truth, and the life. We must completely submit our lives to Christ and allow ourselves to be spiritually led. We need to follow His leading. A *crisis of belief* challenges us to either move forward or to get out of the situation we find ourselves in. These cowabunga leaps of faith contain elements of predictability that are scripturally based, but they also contain surprise elements.

The narrow path that few dare follow is unpredictable because God doesn't tell us where He is leading us, how we'll get to where He is taking us, when we'll get there, how long each new season will last, where our finances will come from, or who we will meet or work with along the way. At some point, we begin to understand that we can't control anything. Instead of driving, we become passengers. Instead of giving directions, we learn how to listen for directions. Instead of telling others what to do, we become servants who are told what to do. The stronger our willpower is, the greater our willpower gets crushed. His soft, tender, nudging love says, "Follow me."

Scripture References

And a great road will go through that once deserted land.
It will be named the Highway of Holiness.
Evil-minded people will never travel on it.
It will be only for those who walk in God's ways;
fools will never walk there.
(Isaiah 35:8)

These gates lead to the presence of the Lord,
and the godly enter there.
(Psalm 118:20)

Jesus told him,
"I am the way, the truth, and the life.
No one can come to the Father except through me."
(John 14:6)

God blesses those who are poor and realize their need for him,
for the Kingdom of Heaven is theirs.
God blesses those who mourn,
for they will be comforted.
God blesses those who are humble,
for they will inherit the whole earth.
God blesses those who hunger and thirst for justice,
for they will be satisfied.
God blesses those who are merciful,
for they will be shown mercy.
God blesses those whose hearts are pure,
for they will see God.
God blesses those who work for peace,
for they will be called the children of God.
God blesses those who are persecuted for doing right,
for the Kingdom of Heaven is theirs.
(Matthew 5:3–10)

Self-Reflection Questions

Am I traveling down the broad highway, or the narrow path that few find?

Do I need God's help to break the bondage of mental strongholds?

Is my faith journey based on self-righteousness, pride, ego, and/or self-centeredness?

Am I completely submitted to Christ, and am I being spiritually led?

Meditate on the scripture verses in this chapter.
How do they apply to my life?

Chapter 11

The Spirit Realm

*We proclaim to you what we ourselves have actually seen and heard
so that you may have fellowship with us.
And our fellowship is with the Father and with his Son, Jesus Christ.
We are writing these things so that you may fully share our joy.
~ 1 John 1:3–4 ~*

I became something like a fish out of water while trying to learn how to follow a subtle new voice that seemed to be speaking impressions into my mind. Since I was in totally uncharted waters, initially it was very awkward. It was like trying to rub my belly in a circular motion while also trying to pat myself on the head. What made things more difficult is that, up until this point, I had never heard anyone talk about having a relationship with Jesus the way that I was suddenly experiencing Him.

The Lord opened my spiritual eyes and ears so that I could see, hear, and experience the spiritual realm. In the natural realm, the way my mind processed information was mostly from past experiences and traditional church services. Suddenly, I was experiencing the supernatural which tapped into unlimited possibilities. My brain kept telling me, "I've never seen that before. That's not real. What I am seeing and hearing is all my imagination. God doesn't speak to people like that. That wasn't God." Later, I learned that doubt and negatively suggestive thoughts came from the antichrist spirit causing confusion within my mind.

I will never forget what happened while I was sitting next to Todd on Sunday, May 11th, 2003. It was just a few weeks after allowing the Lord to actually be my Lord. It was Mother's Day. We were at Riverbend Church, a beautiful church overlooking Lake Austin. Pastor Gerald Mann's sermon was on how difficult it is to be a mother raising children. Suddenly, God's presence came upon me and overwhelmed me and I began weeping. I didn't hear anything that Gerald Mann said after that because Jesus started speaking directly to me through more thought impressions. Jesus said, "I know you're still wondering if all your sins have been forgiven. I know there are many. All of your sins are forgiven."

The Lord was teaching me how to walk, but my initial baby steps were confusing since I didn't know anyone at that time who had similar experiences. Since I attended a Bible study at Riverbend, I decided to set up a meeting with the pastor who taught Bible studies to make sure I wasn't crazy. When I met with Rick, he asked, "What's going on? How can I help you?"

Suddenly, all kinds of words came spewing out of my mouth. I told Rick, "God did this. I heard God tell me that. Then God did this." After I realized that he wasn't going to call the police or have me committed to a mental ward, I told him what happened on Mother's Day. When I finished telling him the story, he smiled at me and said, "James, you aren't losing your mind. God is just speaking to you a lot. God speaks to some people more than others, especially if they have a special calling. Just relax and keep trusting God." When I left Rick's office, another huge burden seemed to be lifted off my shoulders. I remember thinking, "Ok, I am not crazy. Whatever is happening to me is real. I don't know where this will lead, but I am not turning back even if others think I am crazy." I call it crazy faith.

If you have the guts to walk down the narrow path that few follow, others will think you are crazy. At times, you might even question your own sanity which is what brought me back to Rick's office a few weeks later.

Scripture References

Jesus replied, "I have already told you, and you don't believe me.
The proof is the work I do in my Father's name.
But you don't believe me because you are not my sheep.
My sheep listen to my voice; I know them, and they follow me."
(John 10:25–27)

If it seems we are crazy, it is to bring glory to God.
And if we are in our right minds, it is for your benefit.
Either way, Christ's love controls us.
Since we believe that Christ died for all,
we also believe that we have all died to our old life.
(2 Corinthians 5:13–14)

Self-Reflection Questions

Am I walking with, and enjoying the fellowship of God and other Christians?

What adjustments do I need to make to live a Christ-centered lifestyle?

Am I satisfied with religion, or do I want to experience Jesus in a deeper way?

Meditate on the scripture verses in this chapter.
How do they apply to my life?

Chapter 12

The Red Tank Top

Obviously, I'm not trying to win the approval of people, but of God.
If pleasing people were my goal,
I would not be Christ's servant.
~ Galatians 1:10 ~

Two months after my burning-bush-type encounter at Gethsemane Lutheran Church, I found myself bedridden for three straight days. While I slept, God gave me a very clear and vivid dream/vision. Although God had spoken to me numerous times through internal knowings, this was different. In the vision, I saw myself wearing my red tank top, shorts, and sandals to Riverbend Church, which is located in a wealthy part of Austin, Texas. I just knew that I was supposed to wear it four Sundays in a row. Since I attended that church, I knew that the unwritten dress code was semi-formal, if I wanted to fit in with everyone else.

In the vision, I saw the red tank top draped over a clothes hanger that hung from my bedroom door post making it impossible to leave my room without remembering to put it on before going to church. I didn't have any clue why God would want me to wear that outfit to church four Sundays in a row. I just had this internal knowing that was what He wanted. It didn't make any sense at all. What concerned me, even more, was that I couldn't stop thinking about it.

At this point, I was a baby Christian who was two months into learning how to live a sober lifestyle. Change was happening! Because Jesus was very active in my life, several thoughts were crystal clear; He was leading me on an adventuresome journey, and I believed that He had the answers to every problem, situation, or circumstance that I was facing while trying to recapture a life worth living—one filled with meaning and purpose. If God really wanted me to wear a red tank top to church, then I was too afraid not to do it, but I needed to be sure it was the Lord leading me rather than the antichrist spirit tricking me into doing something that would lead to me humiliating myself.

Since I was stuck between a rock and a hard place, I decided to set up another meeting with Pastor Rick. I figured that he would tell me that God wouldn't want me to wear a red tank top, shorts, and sandals to Riverbend Church especially since I have tattoos on both of my upper arms. After listening to my description of the dream/vision, Rick surprised me by simply saying that he didn't know why God would have me do that. Then he surprised me, even more, when he said he couldn't give me any advice about what to do other than to encourage me to keep praying about it. That wasn't the answer that I was looking for since I was hoping that he would tell me that God would never make me do that. Instead, I was left facing a major *crisis of belief*.

While heading towards the exit after meeting with Rick, I noticed that the office door of Pastor Gordon Smith was open. After tapping on his office door, I asked him if he had a few minutes to spare. Gordon invited me to come in and sit down. To my surprise, when I shared the dream/vision with him, hoping that he would give me a different answer, he gave me the same advice that Rick had given. When I left their offices, I was proud of myself for seeking the wise counsel of others, but I was still left facing that major *crisis of belief*.

While praying I began to realize that awareness of God's omnipresence is fairly common. What isn't common is for God to give us directional commands that move us into supernatural spiritual positions filled with grace. Common sense told me not to wear the red tank top because it would attract unnecessary attention along with persecution. My spirit-man recognized Jesus' voice which beckoned me to step forward in faith. Since the spirit of the antichrist attacks our thoughts, learning to recognize Jesus' voice, even if the content of what He is saying is opposed to common sense, trains us in obedience-based decision making, which is the safest way to stay on the narrow path.

I decided to try wearing the outfit one time to church before committing to all four weeks. Back then I was very worried about what others thought, so instead of focusing on pleasing an audience of One (the Lord), I convinced Todd and his girlfriend Katie to meet me in the parking lot so that they could walk on either side of me into Riverbend Church. This way they could shield people from seeing the very large tattoos on my upper arms. I figured with Todd and Katie on either side of me I could be obedient to what I thought God might have asked me to do and minimize the amount of stirring that I faced while testing out if the dream really came from God.

It worked perfectly until Pastor Mann during his sermon encouraged us to get up from our pews to meet and greet the neighbors seated around us before beginning his sermon. When we turned around, an elderly couple seated behind us looked at my appearance with a disgusted look in their eyes. When they did, I felt a strange new connection to Jesus which enabled me to see His earthly ministry from a completely different perspective. I began to understand the connection between persecution, faith, and obedience-based decision making. Right then and there, I decided I wanted to experience more.

I didn't need escorts for week number two. Since my faith had increased, I decided to attend Gordon Smith's Bible study class before church, which was my normal routine. When I did, to my surprise, no one said anything about how I was dressed or my tattoos. Then something unusual happened while walking from Bible study towards the main worship center entrance. The person in charge of the greeters stopped me, told me they were short-handed, and then he asked if I could volunteer as a greeter. Suddenly, there I stood in my red tank top, tattoos on my upper arms, holding the door open while greeting hundreds of people who came to worship.

As people approached the sanctuary, I looked at their facial expressions. The vast majority didn't even notice my tattoos or care about how I was dressed. They were simply grateful that I was holding open the door. A few looked at me with condemning expressions in their eyes which enabled me to experience Jesus in an amazing new way—very different from reading about Jesus in a book written by someone else.

After the second week's experience, I figured I had mastered the lesson that Jesus was trying to teach me. I had faced my *crisis of belief*—fear of persecution—and thought I passed the obedience test. Then, on Saturday, while reading the book of Acts in my living room, God's presence fell upon me. While the glory cloud covered me, I became saturated in joy. The hair stood up on the back of my neck and arms while I was weeping like a baby in God's presence.

I was totally overwhelmed by a new infilling of God's Spirit. While it was happening, I didn't have a clue why. It seemed to last a very long time. When the glory cloud left, I regained my composure. That is when God spoke a thought impression into my mind which enabled me to realize that there was a connection between what just happened and the scripture verse that I was reading before it started.

After I reread Acts 5:41, God spoke plainly to me through the scriptures. God had filled the apostles with joy and a new infilling of the Holy Spirit as a reward for the righteous persecution which they endured. Little did I realize at that point, God was molding and shaping my character to give me the strength to withstand the intense religious persecution that I would face after God gave me the vision to produce the Power of the Cross Festivals at Auditorium Shores, which left me feeling totally rejected, yet also filled with joy.

Scripture References

The apostles left the high council rejoicing
that God had counted them worthy
to suffer disgrace for the name of Jesus.
(Acts 5:41)

Your old men will dream dreams,
and your young men will see visions.
(Joel 2:28)

So be happy when you are insulted for being a Christian,
for then the glorious Spirit of God rests upon you.
(1 Peter 4:14)

The priests could not continue their service because of the cloud,
for the glorious presence of the LORD filled the Temple of God.
(2 Chronicles 5:14)

The Temple was filled with this cloud of glory,
and the courtyard glowed brightly with the glory of the LORD.
(Ezekiel 10:4)

Self-Reflection Questions

If God asked me to do something, would I do what He asked?

Am I more concerned with pleasing others than I am about pleasing God?

When it does not make sense, will I still seek to obey God?

Am I allowing God to mold and and shape my character?

Would I allow God to lead me on a new, adventuresome journey?

Meditate on the scripture verses in this chapter.
How do they apply to my life?

Chapter 13

The Devil Gets Desperate

The temptations in your life are no different from what others experience.
And God is faithful.
He will not allow the temptation to be more than you can stand.
When you are tempted,
he will show you a way out so that you can endure.
~ 1 Corinthians 10:13 ~

On Saturday, June 28th, 2003, I was sitting in my living room praying. At around 10 a.m., God spoke a thought impression into my mind, and said, "Get in your car now and drive to Great Hills Baptist Church." I was a member of Riverbend, not Great Hills, but on this day, God directed me to find a pastor at Great Hills.

As I pulled into the very large complex, I saw scaffolding surrounding the exterior of the church. It looked like they were stuccoing the entire exterior. Then the antichrist spirit spoke a suggestive lie into my thoughts saying, "It's Saturday. They aren't here. You're wasting your time." Although tempted, I resisted the strong urge to turn around and go back home. I continued driving around looking for signs of activity. Just then, I came across a mobile construction trailer. As soon as I pulled up to it, the front door opened and a man walked out. I got out of my car before he got into his, and I said, "Excuse me. I am looking for a pastor." Glenn Rogers, whom I had never met until that moment, said, "I am a pastor and I am the only one here." I grinned and said, "Then you're the one I am supposed to see."

He looked into my eyes, paused, and said, "Ok, follow me inside to my office." When we sat down, he said, "Ok. How can I help you?" I told him about my experience that day. Then he said, "You can go directly to Christ for that?" Then he changed the subject and started talking about my need to get baptized. While he spoke, I shut up and listened. He told me everything that anyone would ever need to know about getting baptized, including why it is important to do it with a committed heart. He also said that anyone could baptize me and that I should do it right away.

When he finally finished talking, I said, "That's interesting that you brought up baptism because God has been speaking to me about that. How did you know I've never been baptized?" Glenn looked at me, puzzled, and then he said, "I thought you asked me about baptism." I just smiled while thanking him for meeting with me.

On Sunday, I went to Gordon Smith's Bible study at Riverbend Church. He spent the entire hour discussing agape love. I had never heard of agape love before even though God's perfect love had become an instrumental part of the healing process which was suddenly being manifested throughout every area of my life.

On Monday morning we had our weekly sales conference call. Before the call ended, I really surprised my boss, Nick, when I announced that I planned to get baptized in two days and that I wanted him to be the one who baptized me.

Nick and I agreed to meet at Riverbend Church later that day to make arrangements. While at the church we bumped into Patrick Abbott who was the church's executive pastor. He suggested that instead of using the normal baptism facility, I should prayerfully consider getting baptized in the stream that runs through Remembrance Gardens, which is a burial ground for church members. It wasn't until later that I began to understand the significance of Pat's last-minute recommendation—God had orchestrated my baptism to be in a garden. Remember the Garden of Gethsemane (Garden of Decision) and its tie to the Lutheran church located off Highway 183 (Highway of Holiness), where I saw that illuminated cross?

While writing this book, the Lord spoke another thought impression into my mind. He said, "Count the days between your birthday and the day you drove down Highway 183 to the place you got baptized, Remembrance Gardens." That is when I discovered that I had gotten baptized exactly 183 days after my fortieth birthday.

On Tuesday, I stopped at a 7-Eleven on what by now had become for me the Highway of Holiness. As I was getting ready to get back into my car, I heard Frank calling my name from an adjacent parking lot. After I walked over to say hello, he explained why he was standing in front of the liquor store. He told me it was the only place that sells a special kind of small cigars. While Frank and I were talking, unbeknownst to him, a temptation came at me hard which caught me totally off guard.

One of the most beautiful-looking women that I've ever seen was suddenly standing in front of me wearing a very low cut and extremely sexy dress. She had gotten out of her car and strutted her stuff intentionally, right in front of me. She paused, lifted up her sunglasses to make sure that I could see her eyes, and combed my entire body with those eyes to make sure I knew that she wanted me.

I was wearing the same red tank top that God had challenged me to wear to church months earlier. I was in great shape back then, so initially, I thought that she was attracted to my muscles and tattoos. What I didn't recognize at the time was that this was a demonic attack sent to cause me to lust. She then walked into the store. When she came out a few minutes later, she did the same thing. She strutted, paused, lifted her sunglasses, scanned my body again, got back into her car, and simply sat there, staring at me. Her alluring invitation beckoned me over.

She said, "Write down my number and call me tonight." I replied by saying, "I am sorry. I don't have a pen." Then she said, "Program my number into your cell. Are you ready?" At this point, I couldn't stand it anymore. I let go of what little restraint I had, and said, "What are you doing now?" She said, "I can't now, but call me tonight after 7 p.m."

Lustful thoughts are fairly common for new people in recovery who are trying to learn how to tame their emotions. I was ready to marry this woman and spend the entire weekend shacked up in a cheap honeymoon suite somewhere. Needless to say, I took her phone number.

Instead of calling her, I drove myself to a recovery meeting at Northland, an alcohol treatment facility with Alcoholics Anonymous meetings. While walking into a meeting, I bumped into Judy. I knew she was a Christian so I told her what happened. She suggested that I read Ephesians 6.

After the meeting, I told another friend, Mike, what happened. To my surprise, he also suggested that I read Ephesians 6, which he said covered spiritual warfare and putting on the full armor of God.

After sharing the story with an older man, he told me that I needed to quit pouring kerosene on the fire and flaming it. Then he said, "Instead of giving lustful thoughts power by talking about what happened, pray for that woman since she was clearly possessed. Then erase her number from your cell phone and get down on your knees and ask God to remove the lust from your thoughts and pray for her salvation."

Scripture References

Keep alert and pray, so that you will not give in to temptation.
For the spirit is willing, but the body is weak!
(Matthew 26:41)

Stay alert! Watch out for your great enemy, the devil.
He prowls around like a roaring lion,
looking for someone to devour.
(1 Peter 5:8)

Teach me to do your will, for you are my God.
May your gracious Spirit lead me
forward on a firm footing.
(Psalm 143:10)

Each of you must repent of your sins and turn to God,
and be baptized in the name of Jesus Christ for the forgiveness of your sins.
Then you will receive the gift of the Holy Spirit.
(Acts 2:38)

Put on all of God's armor so that you will be able to stand firm
against all strategies of the devil.
For we are not fighting against flesh-and-blood enemies,
but against evil rulers and authorities of the unseen world,
against mighty powers in this dark world,
and against evil spirits in the heavenly places.
(Ephesians 6:11–12)

So humble yourselves before God.
Resist, the devil, and he will flee from you.
(James 4:7)

The sinful nature wants to do evil,
which is just the opposite of what the Spirit wants.
And the Spirit gives us desires that are the opposite of what the sinful
nature desires. These two forces are constantly fighting each other,
so you are not free to carry out your good intentions.
(Galatians 5:17)

Self-Reflection Questions

Am I walking in harmony with God, who reminds me of
His omnipresence?

Am I experiencing God working in and through my life?

When the devil attacks my weaknesses, do I give in or do I overcome?

Do I have true accountability partners in my life that I can turn to when
I am tempted or need wise council?

How does Ephesians 6 symbolize the spiritual warfare common
to everyday life?

Meditate on the scripture verses in this chapter.
How do they apply to my life?

Chapter 14

The Best Day of My Life

After his baptism, as Jesus came up out of the water,
the heavens were opened and he saw the Spirit of God
descending like a dove and settling on him.
~ Matthew 3:16 ~

The best day of my life is still when I got baptized—with a committed heart—on July 2, 2003. At 5 p.m. I drove east on Highway 183, right past the same 7-Eleven as the day before, and turned onto Highway 360 South. As soon as I did, a dark Suburban pulled in front of my car and personally escorted me through all kinds of five o'clock traffic to where I needed to exit—the entrance to Riverbend Church's Remembrance Gardens.

During the 20-minute drive, God's presence filled my car. The hair stood up on the back of my neck, and I wept like a baby. Struggling to figure out what was happening to me, I looked closer at the SUV. That is when I noticed that on the back bumper it had a yellow sticker that read, "Agape Love–A Christian Love Thing." On the back windshield, it had another decal of a shield and sword, with the words "Ephesians 6", which symbolizes spiritual warfare and the armor of God.

When I saw those decals, I began to comprehend that God was doing something that was above and beyond all I could think of or even imagine. Three years later, while meeting Bishop Lawrence Wilkerson from Agape Christian Ministries for the first time, I noticed that he drove a dark Suburban with two decals, which looked just like the decals that I remembered from the night I got baptized. The problem was the Agape Love decal was white and I remembered it being yellow. When I told him this story he said, "It was yellow. I recently changed that decal to white." He confirmed, without knowing it at that time, that it was his SUV which God had used to give me a personal escort to my baptism. He also invited me to share this story in front of his congregation one Sunday. (Afterward, Bishop Wilkerson became a member of the advisory board that I put together for the Power of the Cross Festivals in 2006 and 2007.)

The second miracle took place about 30 minutes after the first wonder happened. Nick was waiting for me in the parking lot of Remembrance Gardens so that we could put on our white robes and make our way down to the stream where my friends were waiting to witness my baptism. Two days before, Nick had told me that I might come up out of the water weeping while God filled me with the Holy Spirit. He said, "It's OK to hold onto me if you feel overwhelmed."

I told him, "I want God to kill the old me so please hold me under the water for a long time." I don't remember being submerged underwater, but I do remember coming out of the water gasping for air. I remember looking at Nick and to my surprise, I didn't feel filled with the Spirit. Then we got up and walked out of the stream. After standing around for a few minutes, everyone started walking back toward the parking lot. Two different people asked if I was coming, and twice to my own surprise, I said, "No, God wants me to stay."

When everyone left, I sat down in dismay and cried out to God, saying, "Ok Lord, why am I supposed to stay? Is this all that there is to water baptism? Granted, the escort experience coming here was pretty amazing, but why wasn't I filled with the Holy Spirit when I came out of the water?"

I am not sure if what happened next came from within me, or from the outside, or both; but what I do know is that God's Spirit overwhelmed me again, only this time it was much more intense. I became submerged in God's presence. It was like being in a glory cloud filled with love. I heard God saying, "You are my dearly loved son in whom I am well pleased." Suddenly, I found myself back in the stream, on my knees and shaking, crying out to God. I don't know if I was traversing in the spirit realm or what was taking place, but I do remember that words came out of my mouth faster than I could think. The words were a rapid fire of "thank you for this" and "thank you for that." I was overflowing with God's Spirit, which caused me to praise God in a loving and appreciative way.

I am not sure how long I was in the water. Finally, I crawled back out of it, sat on the shoreline, and collected myself. When I was ready, I walked out of Remembrance Gardens. That is when I saw Mike. He had remained in the parking lot waiting for me while everyone else left. He told me that he wanted to make sure that I was filled with God's Holy Spirit. To this day, I can't help but wonder if Mike was an angel. I never saw him again after he gave me the only photographs which I have of my baptism. On the back of one photo he wrote:

69

I drove to Nick's house to meet up with everyone else who attended my baptism. Nick's wife was kind enough to cook a wonderful celebration dinner. The food and conversations were wonderful. After everyone finished eating, Nick and his wife gave me a very nice plaque with the verse from Jeremiah 29:11. After everyone left, a friend agreed to go with me to Mount Bonnell which overlooks Austin. We arrived about fifteen minutes before sunset. As soon as we sat down, God's presence came upon me for a third time that day and once again this time it was different. I wept while a solid beam of light, which came straight from the sun, shone directly at my chest. I tried touching it, but I couldn't feel it. Then I said, "Can you see that?" Jennifer asked, "See what?" I attempted to touch the sunbeam again, but I still couldn't.

Then the antichrist spirit spoke a suggestive thought into my mind saying, "That isn't God. That is a reflection from your sunglasses. It isn't real. Lift up your sunglasses. See if you see it then." When I lifted up my sunglasses, I realized that I was mimicking what the beautiful woman did days before when she tempted me at the 7-Eleven on Highway 183. While holding up my sunglasses, another thought impression penetrated my mind, will, and emotions.

The Lord inspired me to think, "I am a man of faith. God intended me to see this sunbeam with my sunglasses on. I believe what I am seeing." Then I lowered my sunglass so that they were back over my eyes and exercised faith by telling myself that I believed what I was seeing. I continued looking at the beam, which was still hitting me directly in the chest, until a cloud covered the sun right before sunset. Then the solid beam turned into a beam of particles that still hit me directly in the chest. I sat there weeping until God's presence lifted.

I saw the same beam of light the next day while I was getting gas. I didn't see it again until three years later when I was editing video footage from the first Power of the Cross Festival. Without knowing it, we had captured it on video while taping the Fred Thomas Band. Since I had documented proof, I showed it on Austin Public Access TV during a few of our weekly shows which I co-produced with John Cochran. Since then, I have not seen that solid beam of light. At least, not yet.

The Bible indicates that there are multiple infillings of the Holy Spirit and that the fruit of the Spirit is love, joy, peace, patience, kindness, goodness, faithfulness, gentleness, and self-control. God's overwhelming presence has fallen on me many times. I believe God filled me with faith and hope on April 5th. God filled me with joy during the red tank top church experience, and the Lord filled me with agape love when I was baptized as an adult with a *committed* heart. I am not sure which of those made me a bold witness since I became pretty bold after the first major infilling of God's Holy Spirit.

Scripture References

"For I know the plans I have for you," says the LORD.
"They are plans for good and not for disaster,
to give you a future and a hope."
(Jeremiah 29:11)

And God confirmed the message by giving signs and wonders
and various miracles and gifts of the Holy Spirit whenever he chose.
(Hebrews 2:4)

Now all glory to God, who is able,
through his mighty power at work within us,
to accomplish infinitely more than we might ask or think.
(Ephesians 3:20)

"I baptize you with water,
but he will baptize you with the Holy Spirit!"
(Mark 1:8)

For we died and were buried with Christ by baptism.
And just as Christ was raised from the dead
by the glorious power of the Father,
now we also may live new lives.
(Romans 6:4)

Now all glory to God, who is able,
through his mighty power at work within us,
to accomplish infinitely more than we might ask or think.
(Ephesians 3:20)

But the Holy Spirit produces this kind of fruit in our lives:
love, joy, peace, patience, kindness, goodness,
faithfulness, gentleness, and self-control.
(Galatians 5:22–23)

Three things will last forever; faith, hope, and love -
and the greatest of these is love.
(1 Corinthians 13:13)

Self-Reflection Questions

Do I need to get baptized with a fully committed heart?

What is Agape Love, and how does it apply to my life on a daily basis?

What is the best day of my life?

Did it include God?

Meditate on the scripture verses in this chapter.
How do they apply to my life?

Answering the Call to be Sent

Chapter 15

Signs, Wonders, & More Baptisms

You have heard me teach things that have been confirmed by many reliable witnesses. Now teach these truths to other trustworthy people who will be able to pass them on to others.
~ 2 Timothy 2:2 ~

The Kingdom of Heaven is always operating on the earth. Our job is to recognize what God is doing, and step into opportunities where God invites us to represent His hands, feet, and voice.

One evening I was standing outside a convenience store entrance talking to Pat Trocka, when a car pulled up playing very loud Christian music. The driver got out and left his car running while he went into the store and brought out an eighteen pack of beer. Suddenly, the Lord spoke a thought impression into my mind, "I want you to go speak to him." I looked at Pat and said, "The Lord just told me to go speak to that guy."

When he came out of the store and got into his car, I tapped on his window before he started pulling out. While he rolled his window down, I said, "The Lord told me that He wanted me to speak to you, but He didn't tell me why." The young man said, "I know why. I know what this is about." Then he turned the engine off, got out of his car, and got down on his hands and knees and started repenting. Pat and I didn't need to lead him or say anything. He did an amazing job of repenting all by himself while we stood over him silently praying. While praying, I asked the Lord to reveal to me what, if anything, I was to do next. I didn't sense that the Lord wanted me to follow up with him or do anything other than encourage him to call me if he ever wanted to get together.

One month later, while in the middle of a citywide prayer meeting, I received a phone call from Jared, the man at the convenience store. I don't remember what he said, but I sensed God's Spirit telling me that I needed to get together with him right away because it was urgent. Since I was concerned that he might be suicidal, I asked him to meet me that next day to worship together at any church that he preferred. After he informed me that he wasn't attending a local church, I suggested that we meet at Gateway Church since it was close to where he lived. After the church service was over, I introduced Jared to Pastor John Burke. While they talked, I began praying. I asked the Lord to tell me what to do next. I sensed God's Spirit encouraging me to take Jared to Church Under the Bridge (CUTB), which is a homeless ministry.

While driving to CUTB, Jared and I talked and prayed until we pulled into the parking lot under I-35 and Seventh Street. While praying, I asked the Lord to allow us to be His hands, feet, and voice to others in need. As soon as we got out of the car, God's Spirit drew my attention to a man leaning against one of the large pillars that supports the highway. Then the Lord spoke a thought impression into my mind. I looked at Jared and told him that the Lord just told me that He wanted me to go speak to the young man leaning against the pillar but I also told him that God didn't tell me why. Then I said to Jared, "Follow me, listen, observe, and pray."

After we reached the young man I said, "The Lord told me to talk to you, but He didn't tell me why." The young man, whose name was Tom, told me he knew what this was about. Tom said, "I hate God because He killed my wife." With sensitivity and great compassion, I walked Tom through deliverance for the next thirty minutes. Then Tom got down on his hands and knees and repented. While I led him through the prayer of salvation, I noticed a truck pulling a trailer. On the trailer was a water trough that was spilling water over the sides as it turned the corner. While continuing to pray, I watched it turn another corner and pull right into the parking lot where CUTB was conducting the normal Sunday Homeless Ministry services. I had no idea that they were doing baptisms that day.

While Tom was still on his knees, I said, "See that? That is a baptism trough that was brought here for you to get baptized." Tom looked shocked. Then he said, "I just gave my life to the Lord. I am not ready for that." Then I said, "Yes, you are. There are plenty of examples in the Bible of people getting baptized right after they gave their lives to the Lord. Jesus arranged this divine appointment for you in this Kairos [Greek word meaning "right or opportune"] moment. Now is the perfect time for you to get baptized."

After Tom agreed, I introduced him to Pastor Duane Severance. Then I asked Pastor Duane if I could do the baptismal dunks that day. Duane said yes and then he called everyone forward who wanted to get baptized. About twelve people came forward, including Tom. After Duane recited baptism scriptures and explained their meaning, people stepped forward one by one up onto the trailer and climbed into the water trough. Then I asked them to make a public confession of faith before baptizing them in the name of the Father, the Son, the Holy Spirit, and into the likeness of the death, burial, and resurrection life of the Lord Jesus Christ, whose body is the church. Then, when they came up out of the water, I prayed for them to receive the power of the Holy Spirit.

After I baptized six people, the Lord spoke very clearly to me and told me to step aside so that Jared could take my place. I said to him, "The Lord just told me to get you to take my place." Jared looked startled and said, "I can't do that." I replied, "It's not up to me or my decision. The Lord told me to tell you to take my place." Then I assisted Jared, who took my place. After baptizing his first person, his eyes lit up like a Christmas tree. Suddenly, he understood what it really means to be discipled by a more mature believer and be part of God's Kingdom of Heaven that operates on the earth.

Scripture References

We are witnesses of these things and so is the Holy Spirit,
who is given by God to those who obey him.
(Acts 5:32)

And God confirmed the message by giving signs and wonders and
various miracles and gifts of the Holy Spirit whenever he chose.
(Hebrews 2:4)

"But I will send you the Advocate—the Spirit of truth.
He will come to you from the Father and will testify all about me."
(John 15:26)

Therefore, go and make disciples of all the nations,
baptizing them in the name of the
Father and the Son and the Holy Spirit.
Teach these new disciples to obey all the commands I have given you.
And be sure of this: I am with you always,
even to the end of the age.
(Matthew 28:19–20)

Self-Reflection Questions

When was the last time I risked stepping forward in faith?

Do I recognize God's Spirit which oftentimes works through others?

Is God trying to teach me something through other more mature believers?

Meditate on the scripture verses in this chapter.
How do they apply to my life?

Chapter 16

Walk to Emmaus

Suddenly, their eyes were opened, and they recognized him.
And at that moment he disappeared!
They said to each other,
"Didn't our hearts burn within us as he talked with us on the road
and explained the Scriptures to us?"
~ Luke 24:31–32 ~

All believers are called to be ministers of reconciliation. Not only does God redeem our lives, but He also works through those that He has redeemed to reconcile others.

The greatest stories ever told are the true stories that document God's power working supernaturally through people. His power enables us to overcome tremendous odds or deep personal struggles, such as my childhood wounds, anxiety, fear, self-centeredness, and character issues.

After God called me into a personal relationship with Him, He delivered me from multiple addictions. My recovery from a hopeless situation started when I got down on my hands and knees and prayed for God's intervention. Then, God empowered me so that I could overcome the emotional trauma from my past which was keeping me from becoming whole.

One day, my mother called me to tell me that my first wife had called. Melissa told her that she needed to speak to me right away. I stopped what I was doing and started praying. I sensed that God was setting up another divine appointment, but this one ended up being above and beyond all I could think or even imagine.

I had been praying about cleaning up the wreckage from my past which included a list of the people whom I had harmed emotionally. At the top of the list was Melissa, but I never thought that I would ever be able to make amends to her since we hadn't spoken in many years. I also knew that she had remarried, moved, had an unlisted number, and my number had changed, too. So, at exactly the right time, out of nowhere, she felt led to call my mother's phone number, which she still had. Then she gave her number to my mother and asked her to let me know that she hoped we could talk. In other words, God dropped her phone number into my lap. Praise the Lord!

When I called Melissa, we talked for what seemed like hours although it might have been a thirty-minute conversation. She told me three different times that she wasn't sure why she needed to call me. To her credit, she didn't shame me. Instead, we mostly talked about our faith journeys and I asked for her forgiveness which she gave me before our call ended.

When my conversation with Melissa ended, I realized that God had set up our call as a reward for seeking Him and in order to bring closure which we both needed. I felt so good, I contacted my second ex-wife, Terri, that next day to make amends to her. Then I called Terri's brother, Charlie, who does remodeling work, to get an estimate on the condo that I just bought from Jeanne Butterfield at Re/Max Realtors. At least that is why I thought I set up our meeting. It turned out that God had a different purpose for Charlie and me getting together which would play a significant role in my greater leaps of faith over the course of the next several years.

When Charlie and I sat down to go over his remodeling estimate, I shared some of the amazing stories about how God was reconciling my life. Suddenly, tears welled up in his eyes and then he said, "You need to go on the Walk to Emmaus." I asked him to explain what it was, but Charlie didn't do a good job of explaining it, so I silently prayed, "God, if You really want me to go on this Walk to Emmaus, You're going to have to get somebody else to explain it better."

Two days after Charlie and I met, I drove to meet up with my friend Todd and his girlfriend, Katie, to play golf. After I got out of my car, Katie handed me a booklet called *Walk to Emmaus*. I ask her why she gave me that booklet since neither she nor Todd knew about my conversation with Charlie. Katie said, "A man came to church last month, sat down next to us, handed me that booklet, and got up before services started. He never returned." Katie went on to tell me that she had been intending to give me that booklet for the last month but she hadn't been able to find it until earlier that morning. Talk about an answer to prayer! I now had a booklet in my hand with information about the Walk to Emmaus.

On Sunday, the first song that Riverbend choir director Carlton Dillard conducted was called "Walk to Emmaus." I kid you not. I nearly fell out of my chair. Now, during the short span of three days, I had three separate confirmations that God wanted me to do this, which absolutely blew me away. I knew for sure that God wanted me to go on the Walk, patterned after Luke 24:13–35, but I still didn't have any idea why. Later on down the road, I began realizing that those verses were literally coming alive in my life and that Jesus was showing me that He was walking with me, leading me down the very narrow path that few people find and even fewer follow, through Past Mistakes, Mental Strongholds, the Valley of Despair, Mountaintop Views, and Shipwreck Experiences, all of which are documented in this autobiography.

The next day I called Riverbend's main office. When no one answered the phone, I left the following message, "My name is James Timothy Butt. I am supposed to go on the Walk to Emmaus. Does anyone in the office know anything about it? Can someone tell me how to sign up to go on the Walk? I know that I am supposed to go. Please have someone call me right away."

Kay Dodds called me back the next day and set up a meeting for me with someone a few days later. At that meeting, I learned that the Walk to Emmaus, which other denominations call An Encounter, The Road to Damascus, or Tres Dias, is a four-day, non-denominational spiritual retreat and encounter with Christ which strengthens Christians so that they can become better servants.

God's perfect timing for me took place at Camp Young Judaea in Wimberley, Texas. John Hilgers was the Lay Director for Walk #1092 in September 2003. We spent most of our time in a large room seated around twelve large tables, each named after an apostle.

For four days, we sat at Jesus' feet. We worshiped in spirit and in truth and forgot about the cares of the world. It might have been different for others, but what I witnessed was God's Spirit dropping on everyone who was there, which enabled us collectively to experience a sample of heaven on earth.

During the second day, I noticed that everyone's eyes changed colors. One by one, as each person became filled with God's Spirit, their eyes turned the bluest blue that I've ever seen. Their eyes also became filled with compassion. I couldn't stop staring into everyone's eyes because when I did, I was looking at Christ's eyes. Seriously! I felt naked! I knew that there was nothing that could be hidden from the eyes that could see all the way through me and knew everything about me.

At first, my brain struggled to comprehend what was taking place even though it aligns perfectly with Luke 24:13–35. My knee-jerk reaction was another *crisis of belief*. Then I wondered if God was doing something that only I could see. I looked around the room to try to figure out if others were staring into other people's eyes as I was doing. Finally, I locked eyes with someone else who also looked like a deer caught in the headlights. I asked him what he saw and he seemed to be seeing the same thing as I was. That is when I sensed that God was blessing us with something extra-special.

Everyone's eyes remained baby blue and very compassionate for the rest of the weekend. After the weekend, when the Holy Spirit lifted, I became God conscious of the white light that could be found reflecting off the center of everyone's eyes. When I prayed about what I saw, God revealed to me that his DNA can be found within all human beings. Anyone can become a Christian if he/she chooses to believe and repent. Since then, the Lord has given me a special evangelical anointing that has allowed me to walk hundreds of people through the salvation prayer. Praise the Lord!

I enjoyed the whole Walk experience, but of course, I wanted to see Christ in His entirety. I prayed and pressed in, but throughout the weekend the Lord only allowed me to see His eyes and experience the fruit of His Spirit through the other participants. When it was over, I kept wondering if there was more than what I experienced because I sensed that the Lord brought me on the Walk for another reason. Later, I realized that I was right. The Lord used the Walk to Emmaus to lead me into many other godly experiences such as Kairos Prison Ministry, the Crow Nation, and putting together the Power of the Cross Festivals at Auditorium Shores in downtown Austin.

Scripture References

We can make our plans,
but the Lord determines our steps.
(Proverbs 16:9)

Get rid of all bitterness, rage, anger, harsh words,
and slander, as well as all types of evil behavior.
Instead, be kind to each other,
tenderhearted, forgiving one another,
just as God through Christ has forgiven you.
(Ephesians 4:31–32)

For God was in Christ, reconciling the world to himself,
no longer counting people's sins against them.
And he gave us this wonderful message of reconciliation.
(2 Corinthians 5:19)

And having chosen them, he called them to come to him.
And having called them,
he gave them right standing with himself.
And having given them right standing, he gave them his glory.
(Romans 8:30)

And they have defeated him
by the blood of the Lamb and by their testimony.
And they did not love their lives so much
that they were afraid to die.
(Revelation 12:11)

For God is Spirit, so those who worship him
must worship in spirit and in truth.
(John 4:24)

God blesses those whose hearts are pure,
for they will see God.
(Matthew 5:8)

Self-Reflection Questions

Is the emotional trauma in my past keeping me from becoming whole?

Will I make the hard decisions needed in order to be healed?

Am I willing to make amends to others whom I've harmed?

Have I been redeemed, and am I participating in God's redemption plan?

Would I be willing to go on a four-day retreat if it led to a deep, personal, and extraordinary encounter with Christ?

Meditate on the scripture verses in this chapter.
How do they apply to my life?

Chapter 17

Jumping Off the Income Cliff

*Then he said to the crowd, "If any of you wants to be my follower, you must give
up your own way, take up your cross daily, and follow me.
If you try to hang on to your life, you will lose it.
But if you give up your life for my sake, you will save it."
~ Luke 9:23–24 ~*

**In the beginning, it wasn't easy adjusting to living the sober lifestyle since
I used to deal with unpleasant feelings and emotional pain through denial,
masking issues, and self-medicating, but with Christ's help, I began learning
how to confront problems head-on.**

One day, an accountability partner suggested that I meet with Mary Jo,
a mental health counselor who works with people in recovery. During our
second session, she shocked me when she said, "It's obvious that you hate
your job. Why don't you quit?" I laughed while telling her that she was
wrong. I told her that I loved my job. Then she asked, "What is it that you
love about your job?" I told her I loved working for my boss, Nick Coppolo,
working out of my home office, winning great vacation trips, and making six
figures every year.

Then Mary Jo said, "Here is what I want you to do. Don't do it, but allow
yourself to feel what it would feel like if you called your boss today and gave
him two weeks' notice. Just allow yourself permission mentally to feel what
that would be like and then let's meet again in two weeks."

I listened to Mary Jo's suggestion. I took the time to pray about quitting
and then I allowed myself permission mentally to feel what it would be like
if I quit. Three days later, I called Nick, for real, and overcome my fear by
telling him that I was giving him two weeks' notice.

Nick's response was, "Butt! You can't quit. You're my best salesman! Let
me take you to dinner at Sullivan's Steakhouse so I can talk you out of quitting." Nick is a classy guy. That was his way of showing his appreciation for
my twelve years of faithful service to that company. When I prayed about
leaving my job, what I heard God say was, "Don't worry about money. Just

spend time with Me."

The more time I spent being healed by God, the more I realized how much more healing I needed. I also became conscious that I had been deceived by the worldly matrix system which I had allowed to control my thoughts and define what I thought made me happy. I realized that my entire life needed to change and that nothing was more important than spending time with God to strengthen our relationship.

When I had left Southwestern Publishing Company in 1991, it had taken a headhunter two weeks to help me land the "perfect job" with legal publishing company Matthew Bender which was later acquired by Lexis-Nexis. I ended up working there for twelve years. When I left them, my initial thought was that I would spend one month focused entirely on getting to know Jesus and then I would give my resume to a headhunter who would quickly line me up with my next career move. One month with God turned into two, then three, and before long, four. While praying, I kept hearing Jesus singing verses from all the chapters in the book of the Song of Solomon. I also heard Jesus whispering, "Relax. Don't worry about the cares of this world or getting back to work right now. Just spend time alone with Me, in My presence, and allow Me to heal all your emotional wounds."

In the beginning, my full-time job became sitting at the Lord's feet, worshiping Him, praying, soaking in His presence, and allowing Jesus to renew my mind through His Word and by listening to Christian worship and praise music.

Nine months later my savings account was depleted, and I began to be very concerned about my finances. I kept praying for God to give me the strength and the inspiration to get back to work. Instead, the Lord kept saying, "I don't want you to give your resumé to a headhunter. The only people you can give your resumé to are the pastors at Riverbend Church."

At this point, I assumed that God was calling me to become a pastor, so I gave my resumé to pastors Gordon Smith, Rick Diamond, Bob Lively, and Pat Abbott. I figured that God either already had or would instruct them so that they would know what they were supposed to do to help me become a pastor. But as time went by, they never said or proposed anything, which only added to my confusion. It wasn't until later that I understood that God's calling for my life was broader than getting ordained as a pastor to serve in a denomination or religious institution.

In the interim, I ended up spending a lot more of my time alone in the Valley of Crucified Thoughts, which is where God rearranges our thinking and thought processes so that we are able to receive and understand spiritual wisdom, insight, and kingdom-minded clarity. God also used this time to break apart Mental Strongholds that stood in the way of me becoming God's bond-servant.

More about this in the next chapter.

Scripture References

Don't copy the behavior and customs of this world,
but let God transform you into a new person by changing the way you think.
Then you will learn to know God's will for you,
which is good and pleasing and perfect.
(Romans 12:2)

And everyone who has given up houses or brothers or sister
or father or mother or children or property, for my sake,
will receive a hundred times as much in return and will inherit eternal life.
(Matthew 19:29)

So Elisha returned to his oxen and slaughtered them.
He used the wood from the plow to build a fire to roast their flesh.
He passed around the meat to the townspeople, and they all ate.
(1 Kings 19:21)

Dear brothers and sisters,
I want you to understand that the gospel message I preach
is not based on mere human reasoning.
I received my message from no human source,
and no one taught me.
Instead, I received it by direct revelation from Jesus Christ.
(Galatians 1:11–12)

Self-Reflection Questions

Could I give up income security for a period of time to spend time alone with Jesus, to be in His presence?

What would happen if I asked Jesus to renew my mind?

Am I feeding my soul daily with the richness found in God's word?

Will I make prayer an important component of my everyday life, and not just an afterthought?

Meditate on the scripture verses in this chapter.
How do they apply to my life?

Chapter 18

The Crow Nation – Mission Trip & Bible College

Trust in the LORD with all your heart; do not depend on your own understanding. Seek his will in all you do, and he will show you which path to take.
~ Proverbs 3:5–6 ~

While I was a member of Riverbend Church, there was a large Walk to Emmaus contingency. After I went on my walk, I became part of the Emmaus Reunion Groups. These accountability groups supported each other and sponsored new pilgrims to go on future walks. My email was added to a list which connected us with additional opportunities to grow through experiences like mission trips.

One morning I received an email from Trish Burkett encouraging the Walk to Emmaus Riverbend Church community to go on a short-term mission trip to the Crow Reservation in Montana. It was the first of many over the course of several months. Each time I received another invitation, I quickly hit delete because I didn't believe God would send a white man to a reservation to evangelize. I believed that God was more than capable of reaching Native Americans through other Native Americans.

I had never been on a mission trip. In my ignorance, I thought mission trips were about changing other people. What I didn't realize is that mission trips are as much about changing the people who go on these trips as they are about serving others in mission locations. Later, I realized that God sometimes worked through mission trips to launch me into new ministry callings.

Two weeks before the trip, Trish sent out another email saying that someone backed out which meant that they had an opening which needed to be filled. Trish's email also indicated that half the trip was already paid for since that person's deposit was non-refundable. While reading Trish's email, God spoke a thought impression into my mind, "I want you to go on this trip."

Talk about a *crisis of belief*. I didn't even believe that a trip like this was necessary so I said a quick half-hearted prayer. My prayer was, "God, if I am really hearing Your voice, and You want me to go on this trip, You're going to have to give me a bunch of confirmations. Otherwise, I am not going." By the end of that same day, God gave me all kinds of confirmations.

I called Trish on the phone and set up a meeting with her the following day. When I gave her my check, she handed me a one-inch thick mission trip workbook which we reviewed while drinking coffee. Flipping through it, I came across the history of the Crow Nation. It was then that I realized I was wearing a James Avery necklace which was a replica of the Crow national emblem. The only difference is that it was a slightly different Christian version. Clearly, the James Avery artist used the Crow emblem as inspiration to create the very special necklace which was the only Christian jewelry that I owned. I showed it to Trish and said, "The Lord just gave me another major confirmation that I am supposed to go." Trish simply smiled.

During the week-long mission trip, we worked hard on construction projects during the day and Trish did a wonderful job leading us in nightly discussions about what it means to become servants of Christ. I also became friends with a young Crow man. Towards the end of the week, he and I hitchhiked around the reservation so that we could pass out stuffed animals to hospitals, day care facilities, and visit his relatives.

While we were hitchhiking, I noticed that everyone who picked us up complained about our host church or about other churches in their community. After this happened multiple times, the Lord spoke a thought impression into my mind. The Lord said, "I am calling you to build community among different churches."

Initially, I had no idea what that meant. Looking back now, I realize that is when the Lord began birthing a vision in me for church unity, a vision which ended up consuming the next three years of my life.

In the town of Crow Agency, Montana, there is a church called Spirit of Life Lighthouse for the Nations Foursquare Church. The church's pastor is Kenneth Pretty-On-Top and the associate teaching pastor was Doug. They were starting a two-year Bible college to provide pastors for the Crow Reservation. After Doug told me about it, I couldn't stop thinking about what he said. Since I could not find the passion or energy to get back into being a salesman again, much less any other kind of career, after surrendering my life to Christ, I figured that I needed to get ordained by an accredited religious institution so that I could become a pastor. It appeared like an opportunity which would enable me to pursue the new passion in my life that consumed my thoughts. Little did I know that I would spend many years hoping to get ordained and then when I did, I would find myself ripping up my ordination paper over a spiritual principle that I could not ignore.

I said nothing to the other members of our team about it—I just prayed about it—until a week after we flew home from our trip. Since I was facing another major *crisis of belief*, I sent out an email to our team asking them to join me in prayer. Instantly, one of the guys asked if he could come over to pray with me. It turned out to be more of a lecture than prayer. He believed that I was making an emotional decision which he felt would be a huge mistake. He tried talking me out of going back. Others had mixed advice. Trish encouraged me to keep praying.

One day while I was driving, God's Spirit directed me to stop at a Christian bookstore, pick a random book off the shelf, open it, place my finger on a paragraph, and allow Him to speak to me. The book I chose, which I had never heard of before, was called *The Cost of Discipleship* by Dietrich Bonhoeffer. The quote read;

> "The Cross is laid on every Christian. The first Christ-suffering which every man must experience is the call to abandon the attachments of this world. It is that dying of the old man which is the result of his encounter with Christ. As we embark upon discipleship, we surrender ourselves to Christ in union with his death—we give over our lives to death. Thus it begins; the Cross is not the terrible end to an otherwise God-fearing and happy life, but it meets us at the beginning of our communion with Christ. When Christ calls a man, He bids him come and die."

I've heard people talk about the importance of having faith. I frequently have experiences where God speaks into my life which gives me the faith and grace to move forward. This teaches me how to respond during a *crisis of belief*. This is done by coming into agreement with God's written and spoken words, stepping forward in faith towards where we believe God is leading us, and making adjustments in our lives to align our will with God's will. Then we are able to make any final adjustments necessary to bring us into perfect alignment with His will. This fulfills for us the model prayer that Jesus gave all humanity when He said, "Let thy will be done on earth as it is in Heaven."

Prayer is a process which enables us to wrestle with and overcome carnal thoughts. Included in my *crisis of belief* prayers were some really big mental hurdles which I considered while counting the cost on whether or not I should move.

While praying about attending Bible college on the Crow reservation, which was starting up in less than three weeks, the Lord told me to write down why I thought I couldn't simply move from Austin, Texas to Crow Agency, Montana. Included in my written reasons were the following: 1) I owned a very nice condo. 2) My monthly mortgage was $1200 per month. 3) I owned a Lexus Sports Coupe 400, which wouldn't survive the winters in Montana and it was too small to move my belongings. 4) I owned expensive furniture that was heavy. It would have been hard to move even if I had to put it in storage. 5) My savings account was depleted. Since I wasn't employed, I didn't have any income to pay the $1200 monthly mortgage payments while I would be gone for two years. I thought for sure this last point was a deal breaker since two years' worth of mortgage payments would equal $28,800. However, I did figure out that I could cash in some of my stocks to finance two years of living expenses in Crow Agency.

When I called my family to discuss the decision, they recommended selling my condo. When I talked to my next-door neighbor, Jean Butterfield, she suggested that I pay her a small management fee to rent out my condo. She said, "Since we share a common wall, you know I'll be very picky and make sure I rent it out to a great tenant that is responsible. I'll get them to sign a yearly lease so you only have two rental contract periods."

Again, I found myself in the Valley of Indecision which is where we learn to stretch our faith muscles. It is one of the places where God crucifies our soulish thoughts to perfect our faith, oftentimes by turning our world upside down to teach us what is actually right side up. The Valley of Indecision—and Crucified Thoughts—is where we face our Garden of Decision moments. It is where God's living Word becomes flesh in our own lives—the glory of God radiating through the life of a Christ follower.

God answered my prayers with thought impressions in my mind. God said, "Here is what I want you to do. You are too attached to your car. I want you to get rid of it. As far as your condo is concerned, you don't need to sell it. Let Rob and Lisa Jackson, who are in ministry, live here rent free and you pay the mortgage out of your 401(k). If you will do that, I'll let you keep the rest of your 401(k) for now. As for your furniture, you don't need to move any of it. Let Rob and Lisa enjoy it while you are gone."

Suddenly all obstacles were completely gone. Fear left my soul as well. The same God who spoke the universe into existence spoke to me. It instantly changed everything about my situation, and I was filled with enough faith to move forward with confidence.

I called Rob and Lisa and told them what the Lord told me. Since they were getting ready to move, the timing was perfect. They praised God for their good fortune since my place was much nicer than where they had planned to move. When they asked me how long I'd be gone, I told them, "I can't give you any guarantees but you can stay here as long as I am gone or until God tells me differently." They were elated to move into their new condo a week later, rent-free.

I traded in my Lexus for a Subaru hatchback, then I loaded up my car and drove to Montana. I arrived a few days before Bible school started and moved into an inexpensive furnished apartment in Hardin, Montana, which is on the outskirts of the reservation. Since school didn't start for a few more days, I decided to attend the dance competition at the Crow Fair Pow Wow.

While walking back to my car, I came across a revival tent. I learned the worship team was from Nashville, Tennessee. The third-generation preacher said God had given him a healing anointing. Then he started praying for people and almost all of them fell down. I learned later that this is referred to as being slain in the Spirit.

Up to this point, I had never been exposed to Charismatic, Pentecostal, or Five-fold ministry teachings, so my brain struggled to comprehend what was happening in front of me. I didn't know if it was real or false teaching, so I did the only thing which made any sense. I started praying. My prayer was, "Lord, what is this? Is this real or not? You know my back needs healing but this seems to have a lot of emotion attached to it. I am going to stand here and not move. If You want him to lay hands on me, I'll let him if he walks back to where I am standing."

He never walked back to where I was standing. God didn't speak to me either. I now know that sometimes the best lessons come when God remains silent. I went home that night with a sore back, wondering if I missed a real move of God's Spirit.

The next day while praying, I reflected on what had or hadn't happened the night before. That is when I realized my mistake. I might have missed my healing because I didn't step forward in faith. I also realized that I needed to change my thoughts by becoming more open-minded to any possibility when it came to the things of God. From that moment on, I swore to myself that I would be open-minded to new interpretations, different teachings, and especially open to learning as much as I could about God's Holy Spirit, since the Holy Spirit seems to be the least understood by those of us who call ourselves Christians.

A few days later, classes started at Pastor Kenneth Pretty-On-Top's Spirit of Life Foursquare Church. Nineteen of us started out taking classes but only five of us were considered full-time students.

One day Doug, one of the teachers, stopped by my apartment. He asked me if I had received the gift of speaking in tongues. I asked him what that meant. He asked if I would be interested in learning. I said, "I am open-minded when it comes to God things, and I am especially open-minded to learning more about God's Holy Spirit."

Doug had me open my Bible and then he began showing me New Testament scriptures about speaking in tongues, and the gifts given by Christ to God's church. Then Doug handed me a book written by a pastor who was kicked out of a mainstream church after he started moving by the power of the Holy Spirit. After I read the first book, Doug gave me a second book, which built my faith in the spiritual gifts mentioned in 1 Corinthians 12, Romans 12, and various other places throughout the New Testament.

When Doug sensed that I was ready, he had me open my Bible to 1 Corinthians 14:1 which says, "Follow the way of love and eagerly desire gifts of the Spirit." Then Doug asked me, "Do you eagerly desire all the spiritual gifts that God wants to give you?"

I said, "Yes."

Then he asked me if I would like to speak in tongues. I said, "Yes."

We grabbed hands and then he began speaking in tongues and said (in English), "Allow your tongue to be loosed and follow my lead." When I tried, nothing happened.

Then Doug said, "When you pray in the morning, exercise faith. Tell God that you desire the gift of speaking in tongues."

For the next six mornings, I prayed and tried to speak in tongues but nothing happened. Then, on the seventh day that I exercised faith, God released to me the gift of tongues.

As stated earlier, we started out with nineteen people attending classes. After three months, everyone stopped coming except me. When I asked them how much longer they would put forth the effort just for me, they said, "You made a big commitment to come here, so we will continue this for as long as you are here."

After prayerful consideration, I met with Pastor Pretty-On-Top and Doug and told them that I had accomplished what God sent me up there to do. I told them I believed that it would be better for them if I left so that they could retool their teaching program to make it easier for them to fill pastor vacancies on the reservation. They said they understood. I shared my gracious appreciation for everything they did to help me mature. A few days later Doug and I went out to lunch and said our goodbyes.

Thankfully, I didn't rent my condo like others suggested, or sell it as my family encouraged. I just let Rob and Lisa know that I would be coming home and I was able to get right back into my condo. The transition was fairly easy because we were all submitted to the leading of God's Spirit.

My drive back to Texas from Montana was depressing because I thought I failed since I hadn't gotten ordained. When I got home, I decided that enough was enough and pulled the blinds shut and cuddled up in a little ball on my couch. I told myself that I was done chasing after God and that I was sick and tired of trying to follow God's voice. Then I told myself that from then on, I would focus on embracing my sobriety and living a more normal Christian life.

Years later, when I gained greater spiritual maturity, I was able to look back and realize that the Lord's purposes had prevailed in sending me to Crow Agency. The Lord did not send me to Bible College to get ordained by a religious institution, but to introduce me to spiritual gifts. It was there that I received the Baptism of the Holy Spirit with the evidence of speaking in tongues and was exposed to the ministry of healing through the laying on of hands, which I learned are Biblical. He also used my quiet time alone with Him while traveling down the narrow path that few find and fewer follow to teach me the importance of obedience-based decision making.

Scripture References

May your Kingdom come soon.
May your will be done on earth, as it is in heaven.
(Matthew 6:10)

If any of you wants to be my follower,
you must turn from your selfish ways,
take up your cross daily, and follow me.
If you try to hang on to your life, you will lose it.
But if you give up your life for my sake, you will save it.
(Luke 9:23–24)

Yes, everything else is worthless when compared with
the infinite value of knowing Christ Jesus my LORD.
For his sake I have discarded everything else, counting it all as garbage,
so that I could gain Christ and become one with him.

(Philippians 3:8–9)

It is not that we think we are qualified to do anything on our own.
Our qualification comes from God.
He has enabled us to be ministers of his new covenant.
This is a covenant not of written laws, but of the Spirit.
(2 Corinthians 3:5–6)

Let love be your highest goal!
But you should also desire the special abilities
the Spirit gives - especially the ability to prophesy.
(1 Corinthians 14:1)

There are different kinds of spiritual gifts,
but the same Spirit is the source of them all.
(1 Corinthians 12:4)

It is God's privilege to conceal things
and the king's privilege to discover them.
(Proverbs 25:2)

You have been believers so long now
that you ought to be teaching others.
Instead, you need someone to teach you again
the basic things about God's word.
You are like babies who need milk and cannot eat solid food.
(Hebrews 5:12)

So let us stop going over the basic teachings about Christ again and again.
Let us go on instead and become mature in our understanding.
Surely, we don't need to start again with the fundamental importance
of repenting from evil deeds and placing our faith in God.
You don't need further instruction about baptisms,
the laying on of hands, the resurrection of the dead,
and eternal judgment.
(Hebrews 6:1–2)

Self-Reflection Questions

Will I allow myself to be more open-minded to any possibility when it comes to the things of God, keeping my mind open towards the gifts of the Holy Spirit?

Do I trust the Holy Spirit, or do I place more trust in men to help me interpret scriptural truths?

How do I make a decision to follow Jesus?

Do I come into agreement with God's spoken words, step forward in faith, and adjust my life to realign my will to His?

Am I willing to go on a short-term mission trip to experience servanthood?

Is the cost of discipleship too much, or am I willing to pay the price to experience deep intimacy with Christ Jesus?

Chapter 19

Brotherly Love
& Accountability Partners

Let us think of ways to motivate one another to acts of love and good works.
And let us not neglect our meeting together,
as some people do, but encourage one another,
especially now that the day of his return is drawing near.
~ Hebrews 10:24–25 ~

When I returned from Crow Agency I felt lonely, confused, disoriented, and pretty much an all-around wreck. To make matters worse, I sensed that the Lord was withholding His presence from me. I felt uncomfortable going back to the last Austin church I had attended because I felt like a failure for coming home without being ordained.

I decided to go to a recovery meeting at the Northland Group instead of joining a new church. As soon as I walked through the doors, the Lord connected me with Dicky, a man with long term sobriety, who is a very solid Christian through whom the Lord worked to help me regain my composure.

After mentoring me for weeks, Dicky took me to an old graveyard not far from Northland. As we drove through the gates, he said, "Look for God and tell me when you see Him in the things that you notice in the cemetery." Then he took me to one particular grave that had a bench in front of it. We sat down and then he said, "Take your time, look around, and tell me what you see."

After ten minutes of praying, I told him everything I noticed from a spiritual perspective. When he was satisfied that I was where I needed to be, Dicky had me get down on my knees to re-confess my commitment to Jesus as being Lord over every area of my life. With his help, I was back on track to hearing God's voice again with renewed confidence. That is when I realized that I had survived the Montana test.

The best way to regain our spiritual equilibrium is to get help from others.

The best way to maintain our spiritual equilibrium is to help others. I met Curtis at a recovery meeting a few days later. A few months after I started discipling him, it also became very clear that Curtis was ready to give his life to the Lord, so I brought him to that same graveyard.

Driving through the gates, I said, "Look for God and tell me when you see Him in the things you notice here." Then I took Curtis to the grave with the bench. After we sat down, I said, "Take your time, look around, and tell me what you see."

Curtis told me everything he saw, so I asked him if he was ready to ask Jesus to become his Lord and Savior in every area of his life. He looked confused and indecisive, so I suggested that he walk around and pray about whether or not he was ready to make the most important decision in his life.

While Curtis walked around, Lucinda called me. We talked about Crow Agency for about 10 minutes. While we were talking, I noticed that Curtis had wandered off and a car was pulling up about 30 yards from the bench where I was sitting. A lady got out of her car and retrieved flowers from the back seat. Suddenly, God spoke a thought impression and said, "This person is here for Curtis. You need to get off the phone." I told Lucinda, "God just showed up to meet the person I am with. I need to go. I'll talk to you later."

After I hung up the phone, the lady started walking in my direction instead of toward the hundreds of other graves in the immediate vicinity. My prayer became, "God, help me help Curtis. I don't know how to lead him to You or what to say."

I looked up, and the woman was suddenly standing right next to where I was sitting. She asked me if I was a relative of the person whose grave I was sitting in front of. I told her that I was just sitting there to pray. When I asked her why she was there, she said, "To visit my grandmother's grave."

While we were talking, Curtis suddenly appeared standing next to me. She looked at Curtis and asked who he was. After we told her that we were both in recovery, she told us that her husband had over twenty-five years of sobriety. Then she looked at Curtis and said, "It's really simple if you learn how to turn your will and your care over to God as you understand Him." While she said that, I noticed that Curtis's jaw dropped. He recognized that God had just intervened in what we were there to do. Then she walked back to her car and left.

Smiling, I looked at Curtis, and asked, "Now are you ready to give your life to God?" Smiling back, he said, "Yes, definitely!"

I needed Dicky's help, and Curtis needed my help. But it was the Lord's Spirit who set up these divine appointments which restored stability to my journey of faith down the narrow path that few find and even fewer follow.

Scripture References

The eyes of the Lord search the whole earth in order to
strengthen those whose hearts are fully committed to him.
(2 Chronicles 16:9)

Share each other's burdens,
and in this way obey the law of Christ.
If you think you are too important to help someone,
you are only fooling yourself.
You are not that important.
(Galatians 6:2–3)

As iron sharpens iron, so a friend sharpens a friend.
(Proverbs 27:17)

And the disciples went everywhere and preached,
and the Lord worked through them,
confirming what they said by many miraculous signs.
(Mark 16:20)

Self-Reflection Questions

Am I actively participating in the Kingdom of Heaven that operates now on earth?

Have I formed relationships with other believers to grow in love and good works?

Do I have accountability partners to help protect me from making bad decisions?

Is my focus self-centered or blooming in the service of helping others?

Meditate on the scripture verses in this chapter.
How do they apply to my life?

Chapter 20

My "Perfect Job" is Sacrificed

*"So don't worry about these things, saying,
'What will we eat? What will we drink? What will we wear?'
These things dominate the thoughts of unbelievers,
but your heavenly Father already knows all your needs.
Seek the Kingdom of God above all else, and live righteously,
and he will give you everything you need."
~ Matthew 6:31–33 ~*

After I came back from Montana, I found myself at another major fork in the road. The sign on my right read, "Trust God Completely." The sign on my immediate left read, "Trust Common Sense." Then my focus shifted to in between the two signs which locked me into a spiritual position similar to an engine that becomes seized or a deer looking into a truck's headlights in the pitch blackness of night. This is the sign that was planted at the fork in the road:

Did Jesus want me to interpret Matthew 6:31–33 literally, figuratively, or in some other way? That question separated my spirit from my flesh, right down the middle of my entire being.

One of the least understood aspects of Christianity is the battle that takes place between a person's soul and the sanctification work done through the indwelling work of God's Holy Spirit. There are times in every believer's life when God orchestrates shipwreck moments when "all or nothing decisions" are made. Usually, we come upon these monumental moments, which break apart mental strongholds when we find ourselves in the Valley of Blood, Sweat, and Tears. For Jesus, this moment was in the Garden of Decision when He was deeply grieved to the point of death. He fell to the ground and cried out to God the Father, to whom He had submitted His earthly life, and said, "If it is possible, please don't make Me follow this path any longer because it is crushing My mind, will, and emotions to the point of My fleshly death, but if it isn't possible to accomplish Your will through Me unless I go through with this, then let Thy will be done so that You will be glorified through My resurrected life" *(my paraphrase of Matthew 26:37–39).*

The battle being played out over and over again in my mind, will, and emotions was, "Would God really take care of all my needs if I focused on spending time in God's presence so that I could learn how to live a righteous life?" Should I trust God or trust my common sense? The other question troubling my soul had to do with the term "resurrection life." Then, after many dark nights and restless days in the Valley of Indecision and Double-Mindedness, the Lord opened up a supernatural door to test me so that I could learn a very important lesson about myself. God gave me an option, now that I had gained sobriety, to exchange my new life for my old life as a very successful salesperson, making great money and living a very comfortable lifestyle.

Kirk Massey, the owner of the Medical Equipment Group, called me out of the blue. It was the first time I had spoken to him in over twelve years. He offered me a job selling Matrix medical equipment to doctors. What caught my attention was what seemed like his perfect timing. By now my savings account was completely depleted and I still hadn't given out my resume to anyone except the pastors of Riverbend Church.

The Spirit led Jesus into the desert to be tempted by the devil. I now realize that the Lord had allowed the devil to tempt me with the "perfect" job. Kirk offered me the perfect job that satisfied every question that Mary Jo had asked me during our counseling session. Kirk told me that I could be my own boss, work out of a virtual office, set up my own schedule, take off whenever I wanted, and he said that I could make six figures. Talk is cheap, so he also let me know that Clint Fowler, another friend I knew from our Southwestern days, worked for him, and Clint was making really great money.

Suddenly, I had an opportunity to go back to work, which seemed to be one of the only major things missing from a really great life. At least that was my initial perception. Since then I've learned the hard way that my initial perceptions about what God is orchestrating aren't always correct. In fact, oftentimes they are wrong since God wants us to continually seek His face rather than a religious formula.

Initially, after quitting my job, my game plan was to spend thirty days exploring my new relationship with Christ. That turned into an amazing journey but included many restless nights tossing and turning because I believed that I needed to get back to making money again. I would later learn, through the wisdom of hindsight, that God's ways are far superior to my limited understanding. I also discovered through lessons like this one that God's wisdom is beyond human comprehension and I don't have a clue what is best for me because I can't see into the future and God can.

After I accepted the job, I spent weeks studying the sales literature and recordings that Kirk mailed me. During that time, Dicky moved in with me for a few months because he needed a place to stay. He had a hip injury which made it hard for him to work, so I treated Dicky's injury using my demo Matrix Unit. Dicky's hip improved, which increased my salesmanship confidence.

I set up a few clinical demonstrations. Kirk came down to Austin to assist me. We ended up selling one of the $40,000 units which enabled me to pocket about $5,000. A few weeks later I sold two units in one week and profited about $10,000. I can remember thinking that I was back in the saddle again, making great money just like the old days, only now I had gained sobriety which meant that I could be even more successful.

Then, during my morning worship, God spoke a thought impression into my soul calling me back to Him. What God whispered into my ear shattered my heart into a million pieces. My Lord said, "You can go back to being a salesman again if you really want to or you can pack up your demo Matrix Unit and ship it back to Kirk today and tell him that you have been called to follow Me."

My heart was filled with amazing joy and sorrow, both at the same time. My thoughts returned to the fork in the road, that deer standing frozen in the truck's headlights, and the scripture verses that had pierced my heart. The question before me, once again, during this "Garden of Decision" was, "Did Jesus want me to interpret Matthew 6:31–33 literally, figuratively, or in some other way?"

I found myself facing a huge financial *crisis of belief!* Earlier in the week, Dicky had been excited for me when I shared with him that I made two sales worth about $10,000 in commission. When I told him what God shared with me during my morning worship, Dicky said, "It sounds like an easy decision to me. If God told you to do something and you believe in your heart that it is what you are supposed to do, then you need to pack up your demo unit and send it back today." I did it.

I had learned that the Lord wanted me to take Him literally, that His word meant exactly what He said. But still, I had no idea how God was going to provide for all my needs without a steady income. The three sales had replenished my depleted savings account. I could live to die another day while continuing to travel down the narrow path that few find and fewer follow, purifying my mind, will, and emotions.

Right after I sent back my demo unit, I found myself being ridden like a stallion being broken by its trainer. A bit was placed in my mouth and a saddle was strapped onto my back and then my master began riding me. During this stage, the Lord broke my pride and ego, and He removed what strength I had left through a series of lessons that included great suffering, tremendous spiritual warfare, total isolation, an empty bank account, and religious and political persecution.

While I was being broken, I often thought about the decision that I made when I gave up the perfect job so that I could continue to follow Christ. During many sleepless nights, I wondered if I had made the right decision. It wasn't until much later that I finally realized that everything that God had brought me through was really for my own good. I was finally at a place where I understood what Jesus meant when He said, "The gateway to life is very narrow and the road is difficult, and only a few ever find it" (Matthew 7:14).

Scripture References

By his divine power,
God has given us everything we need for living a godly life.
We have received all of this by coming to know him,
the one who called us to himself
by means of his marvelous glory and excellence.
And because of his glory and excellence,
he has given us great and precious promises.
These are the promises that enable you to share his divine nature
and escape the world's corruption caused by human desires.
(2 Peter 1:3–4)

I once thought these things were valuable,
but now I consider them worthless
because of what Christ has done.
Yes, everything else is worthless when compared
with the infinite value of knowing Christ Jesus my LORD.
For his sake I have discarded everything else,
counting it all as garbage,
so that I could gain Christ.
(Philippians 3:7–8)

But Jesus told him,
"Anyone who puts a hand to the plow and then looks back
is not fit for the Kingdom of God."
(Luke 9:62)

At this point many of his disciples turned away and deserted him.
Then Jesus turned to the Twelve and asked,
"Are you also going to leave?"
Simon Peter replied, "LORD, to whom would we go?
You have the words that give eternal life."
(John 6:66–68)

Self-Reflection Questions

Am I stuck living in The Valley of Indecision and Double-Mindedness?

Is my number one priority in life the Kingdom of God and His righteousness?

Would you trust God to provide for you if He called you to leave all to follow Him?

Am I committed to pursuing "The Narrow Path that Few Find"?

Which way will you turn when you reach your John 6:66 Moment?

Meditate on the scripture verses in this chapter.
How do they apply to my life?

Being Equipped
& Crucified

Chapter 21

The Birthing of a Vision

This vision is for a future time.
It describes the end, and it will be fulfilled.
If it seems slow in coming, wait patiently,
for it will surely take place.
~ Habakkuk 2:3 ~

As I said, during my first few months back from Crow Agency, I stopped going to church. Instead, I attended recovery meetings and helped new people in recovery. Occasionally at those meetings, I bumped into Greg. Each time I did, he kept inviting me to check out Gateway Church.

Greg told me that Gateway played rock and roll worship music, which really intrigued me. He was persistent, but curiosity is what finally got the better of me. I decided to go with him at least once so that I could hear what Christian rock and roll music sounded like. I ended up going back a few more times which surprised me since I felt like I was a mature Christian now and Gateway was a seeker friendly church. By that I mean its services were designed for people who were learning to become believers.

After attending four weeks in a row, I decided I needed to find a different church but I didn't have a clue where, so I began praying for God to give me direction. While praying, I heard the Lord say, "I want you to plant the Walk to Emmaus movement at Gateway Church." Silently I thought to myself, "How can I do that? I am brand new here. No one knows me. How could a nobody like me plant that here?" You see, I was still trying to make things happen and control outcomes, and I was still leaning on my own understanding rather than seeing things from God's perspective.

Before the service, they announced that the church was providing a free dinner for anyone who was interested in meeting Gateway's leadership team and to learn more about the vision they had for the community which included a new church building.

When I arrived for dinner, I was seated at a table with six other people. To my immediate left was Nate Echelberger. While conversing with Nate,

I learned that Gateway Church had been birthed out of his house. I also found out that his wife was on staff and that Nate was very active in organizing opportunities to help the men's ministry grow. When I asked him if he'd ever heard of the Walk to Emmaus, his eyes lit up, and he asked me to tell him everything I knew about it. He explained that he had a great friend that had been trying to sponsor him to go on a Walk for some time. When I finished sharing, he said, "I am definitely going now that we've had this conversation."

Since Nate was a founding member of the church, I figured my role in planting the Walk at Gateway Church was now fulfilled. When I prayed for God to release me from attending Gateway, the Lord spoke another thought impression into my mind. This time God said, "I want you to stay at Gateway and get the Senior Pastor, John Burke, to go on the Walk."

The following week, while praying, the Lord said, "I want you to get two Senior Pastors from two different churches to have lunch with John Burke to explain to him how the Walk develops church leadership." Then the Lord said, "I want you to set up a meeting between John Burke, Bill Henderson, and Rick Diamond."

I knew Rick as a Senior Pastor at Riverbend Church, where I had been attending when I had done the Walk, but had only met Bill once, briefly, while attending a Northwest Hills United Methodist Church service where he served as Senior Pastor.

While I was in Montana, Rick had formed a new church, but I couldn't find what they named it. I called Kate Dodds and others who I thought would know, but no one knew the church name, or how I could get in touch with Rick, so I finally gave up looking. Bill's church was right down the street from where I was living, but I felt led to wait on God's reassurance before I met with Bill.

One morning, a few weeks later, I woke up and God said, "Today is the day. I want you to go see Bill Henderson." Suddenly, I had the faith needed to take action. While driving down the street, I just knew that our meeting would take place which, among other things, would confirm that I was hearing God's voice clearly. When I arrived at his office, his personal assistant informed me that he was in a meeting. Surprised, I left my number and asked her to have him call me because I needed to meet with him right away. To make sure I didn't miss his call, I kept my phone next to me at all times. Then, at 5 p.m. sharp, I got a voice mail message from Bill saying he was sorry he missed me and that he was leaving for the day. I couldn't believe I had missed his call. Suddenly, I found myself doubting whether or not I was hearing God's voice to begin with.

That evening, I met my Gateway home group at Rudy's BBQ restaurant on Highway 183. While waiting in a very long line to purchase food, I noticed that the person behind me looked like Bill Henderson. I wasn't exactly sure what Bill looked like, since we only met once for a brief moment, so I said, "Excuse me, but you wouldn't happen to be Bill Henderson, would you?" Bill smiled and laughed, then I told him this story. He confirmed why a Senior Pastor needs to talk directly to another Senior Pastor on the importance of the Walk to Emmaus. Then he agreed to have lunch with John Burke if I would set up a meeting.

When I got home that night, I had received an email that was a forward of a poem from Rick which incorporated the rainbow, which is the symbol for the Walk to Emmaus. It contained all of Rick's contact information and the name of his new church. I called Rick the next day, told him this story, and he agreed to have lunch with John Burke if I set up the meeting.

God was laying the groundwork for a bold move to draw together the churches in the Austin area, but I had no clue at the time what was going on. I just knew that God was orchestrating something which appeared to be a meeting between three pastors related to the Walk to Emmaus.

I had the confirmations I needed to move forward, but prayer revealed that God wanted me to be sensitive to His perfect timing. So, instead of trying to meet with John Burke right away, I sent an email to Bill and Rick and asked them to join me in praying for God to let me know when I should share this information with John. Rick replied back and told me that he was proud of me for waiting. Initially, I figured it might take a few weeks max. After two months passed, I sent another email out to update Rick and Bill so that they knew I was still waiting on God to tell me when to meet with John Burke.

Meanwhile, I went on a local mission trip through Gateway Church, which was held at Mission Impossible in east Austin. They called the three-day weekend "The Urban Submersion." We checked in Friday afternoon and prayed for people at the ARC (Austin Recovery Community) and Salvation Army. On Saturday we worked on restoring a broken-down home in east Austin. Then we attended the Sunday morning worship service at Greater Mount Zion Church. Finally, we served at Church Under the Bridge until late Sunday afternoon. I didn't know it then but God worked powerfully through this local mission trip to line-up critical divine appointments which paved the way for me to set up a nonprofit called "United in His Love."

At Greater Mount Zion Church, I listened to Pastor Gaylon Clark's sermon. While he was preaching, the Lord said, "Gaylon is one of twelve leaders who will have a great impact on what happens in the Greater Austin

Church Community." After God spoke, my immediate response was, "I can see that for sure. Who are the other eleven?" God didn't answer me, but He later led me to each of them separately.

Later that morning I spoke with Pastor Duane Severance at Church Under the Bridge. He was well known throughout Greater Austin as Austin's homeless minister. I was amazed at his patience, generosity, and heart for the homeless. Later, after serving alongside him, we became friends and accountability partners.

As I was waiting on God to tell me when to meet with Pastor John Burke, I attended two Sunday services at Greater Mount Zion Church. Then, to my surprise, Pastor Gaylon's assistant contacted me and said that Gaylon wanted to set up a meeting with me personally. Intrigued, I said yes.

While all this was happening, I participated in the National Day of Prayer at Gateway Church. While I was praying, God said, "Today is the day. I want you to talk to John Burke about the luncheon meeting." John had been the leader over our session. When it ended, he stood up and thanked everyone for coming. Then I went up to him and told him that I needed to speak to him privately.

After we found a quiet area to talk, I shared with John that God wanted him to meet with Senior Pastors Bill Henderson and Rick Diamond to talk about the importance of planting the Walk to Emmaus experience at Gateway. Then I told him that they already agreed to meet with him and that we were waiting for him to say yes before I coordinated the date. He asked me when they had agreed to meet with him. I told him three months ago. A puzzled look came across John's face before he asked me why I waited so long to tell him. I simply smiled and said, "We have been waiting on God's perfect timing." John told me he would look at his calendar and have his administrative assistant get back in touch with me to schedule a date for their luncheon.

While waiting for John to get back with me, I met with Gaylon Clark. When I walked into his office, Gaylon asked if we could hold hands and pray together. When we finished praying, he opened his eyes and looked at me and then he said, "Tell me the vision that God gave you." I didn't know that was why I was there, but after his prompting these words tumbled out of my mouth, "Three pastors are going to get together for lunch to talk about the Walk to Emmaus and building unity in the body of Christ." Suddenly Gaylon said, "I am going."

After he said that, I began praying silently. My prayer was, "God, he just invited himself to the meeting you are setting up that was supposed to only be between three pastors." Then Gaylon went on to say, "I've heard about the

Walk to Emmaus, so I definitely want to attend that meeting." After that, I didn't know what else to say. So I said, "Let me set up the meeting and get back in touch with you."

God expanded the size of the meeting and my perception of the vision. Instead of three Senior Pastors meeting for lunch, the Spirit led me to co-ordinate a luncheon for twelve. Pastor Bill Henderson shared how the Walk helps develop laymen so that they become church leaders and Lee Haley and I shared ideas which connected the Walk to putting together a festival that built unity among the Greater Austin churches. Out of that meeting, the idea for the Austin United Music Festival was birthed which later became the Power of the Cross Festivals.

I didn't know anything about Christian music festivals, but Lee Haley did. One time he had promoted a festival that raised money for a young woman who needed a kidney transplant. Lee connected us to Greg Carnes Productions, owner of HM Magazine, a Christian rock and heavy metal publication, and the local K-LOVE radio station. Right away everything fell into place including sponsorship and radio promotion. We also had a church venue lined up halfway between Austin and San Antonio that would host our Christian festival at their location for free. Everyone insisted everything was perfect, but I felt convicted in my spirit that everything was wrong. What they lined up wasn't what God was calling me to do.

I walked away from it. I walked away from the resources that seemed to be needed to put together what appeared to be a huge Christian music festival. I figured I must have heard God wrong and that the idea of building a unity festival was over since I knew that I didn't have a clue how to put one together by myself. I set down the vision, turned my back, and walked away. To my surprise God had me pick it back up again, only this time totally dependent on Him and not on other people.

By the way, Nate Echelberger from Gateway Church and others ended up going on the Walk. Over the years, God also connected me to other endeavors through the Walk which is really a metaphor for the narrow path that few find and even fewer follow.

Scripture References

Then the two from Emmaus told their story of how
Jesus had appeared to them
as they were walking along the road,
and how they had recognized him
as he was breaking the bread.
(Luke 24:35)

Can two people walk together without agreeing on the direction?
Indeed, the Sovereign LORD never does anything
until he reveals his plans
to his servants the prophets.
(Amos 3:3, 7)

When the Spirit of truth comes,
he will guide you into all truth.
He will not speak on his own but will tell you what he has heard.
He will tell you about the future.
(John 16:13)

Self-Reflection Questions

Am I willing to step outside my comfort zone to experience God?

When was the last time I took a personal risk to experience the Kingdom?

Am I willing to go on a mission trip to experience God in a new way?

Is my prayer life strong enough to hear God's invitation to partner with Him?

Do I see His divine appointments and timing?

Do I follow His voice?

Meditate on the scripture verses in this chapter.
How do they apply to my life?

Chapter 22

Spiritual Gifts

It is impossible to please God without faith.
Anyone who wants to come to him must believe that God exists
and that he rewards those who sincerely seek him.
~ Hebrews 11:6 ~

After I went on the Urban Submersion mission trip, I found myself rotating where I worshiped. I split my time between Gateway Church, Greater Mount Zion, and Church Under the Bridge (CUTB). I was particularly drawn to God's anointing which I saw flowing through Pastor Duane Severance, so I started spending more time serving with him.

When I showed up on May 15, 2005, Pastor Duane announced something different. Then he rolled out a red carpet and placed a microphone in the middle of it. Afterward, Pastor Duane spoke into the microphone and said, "In recognition of it being Pentecost Sunday, I am opening up the microphone so that whoever feels led can come up and pray for our country, city, or anything you feel led to pray." Then God spoke to me and said, "I want you to pray in tongues right now at Church Under the Bridge."

First off, talk about a major *crisis of belief*. To the best of my knowledge, no one had ever spoken in tongues at CUTB. Pastor Duane came from a Baptist background, not Pentecostal. Second, church doctrine clearly states that no one should speak publicly in tongues unless someone with the gift of interpreting tongues is present. At that time, I didn't know anyone, anywhere, and especially at CUTB, who knew how to interpret someone else speaking in tongues.

One by one, people came forward to pray. While they were praying, my flesh battled the leading of God's Spirit. I heard the devil speaking doubt into one ear and the Lord speaking faith into the other. God said, "I want you to go up there and pray in tongues." The devil said, "There isn't an interpreter here and no one has ever spoken in tongues here. You just want to get up there to show everyone that you can speak in tongues."

For twenty minutes a major battle took place between my ears while I tried to decide what to do next, which included doing nothing. Finally, after Pastor Duane said, "We have time for one to two more prayers," I jumped up and walked forward in obedience and faced another "Garden of Gethsemane" decision.

I stood at the open mic, looked at all the people seated in front of me and the hundred people standing behind them, closed my eyes, and let God's Spirit speak through me to communicate to those in attendance. I am not sure how long I spoke in tongues. It felt like forever. When I was done, after seeing the stunned look on Pastor Duane's face, I bowed my head and walked back to my seat. I wanted to hide especially after Pastor Duane walked up to the mic and began following the biblical protocol to correct me since no interpreter was there. He began by saying, "I need to bring correction to what just happened."

Suddenly, someone I had never seen interrupted him. He tapped the pastor on the shoulder and told him God had given him the interpretation for the tongue that was just spoken. Then Pastor Duane stepped aside, and the man gave the interpretation for the prayer that I had just made. What he shared confirmed the vision that God had given me while in Montana, the vision of bringing Austin pastors together for a unity festival. He then walked over to me and said, "Who are you? My name is Brian Lohse. That was cool how God spoke through you and gave me the interpretation."

Brian visited with me for a little while. Then he asked me if I had ever been to a prophetic ministry before. My response was, "What's that?" Brian proceeded to ask me if I knew anything about the teachings of the Five-fold ministry. Again, my response was, "What's that?"

You see, up until this leap of faith in 2005, I didn't know anything about what many consider (because of their lack of knowledge on this topic) to be the black sheep body part of Christ's church. You know, one of the parts that make up the glorious church that is supposed to be without a spot or wrinkle or any other blemish (See Ephesians 5:27).

Brian said, "I believe the Lord has a prophetic word for you that he wants to give you tonight at Glory House." He gave me the address of Glory House Prophetic Ministries. Suddenly, my obedience and God's faithfulness opened up a new door for spiritual equipping which I would need so that I could continue down the narrow path that few find and fewer follow.

Scripture References

I wish you could all speak in tongues,
but even more I wish you could all prophesy.
For prophecy is greater than speaking in tongues,
unless someone interprets what you are saying
so that the whole church will be strengthened.
(1 Corinthians 14:5)

There are different kinds of spiritual gifts,
but the same Spirit is the source of them all.
There are different kinds of service,
but we serve the same LORD.
God works in different ways,
but it is the same God who does the work in all of us.
Spiritual gifts are given to each of us so we can help each other.
(1 Corinthians 12:4–7)

Obey me, and I will be your God,
and you will be my people.
Do everything as I say, and all will be well!
(Jeremiah 7:23)

Self-Reflection Questions

Does my life reflect and point others towards a lifestyle based on faith?

Am I constantly seeking God daily with all my heart, soul, and being?

Have I studied, mediated on, and exercised faith regarding spiritual gifts?

Is my theology based on the teachings of man, or scripture interpreted by the Holy Spirit ?

Meditate on the scripture verses in this chapter.
How do they apply to my life?

Chapter 23

A Spiritual Father

&

the Five-fold Ministry

*Do not neglect the spiritual gift you received through the prophecy spoken
over you when the elders of the church laid their hands on you.*
~ 1 Timothy 4:14 ~

*So, Brian Lohse invited me to Glory House. During my first visit, which
was a men's meeting, they prophesied over me, and then Jim Mihlhauser, who
was standing behind me, prayed over me. While he was praying, my spirit man
leaped within me. Instantly, I sensed that one of my prayers had just been answered. I knew that whoever Jim was, God wanted me to be in relationship
with him. You see, during that season of my life, I had been praying for the Lord
to connect me to a spiritual father figure who could mentor me.*

I started attending the men's meeting with Jim Mihlhauser teaching our
group using Derek Prince's teachings. Derek Prince was a friend of Jim's
who had written fifty-plus books on spiritual gifts, deliverance, and other
Five-fold ministry teaching subjects. After the meeting, I approached Jim
and we prayed together and a few days later he agreed to take me under
his wing to mentor me. Prophet Jess Bielby had been invited by the Glory
House pastor, Mark Henderson, to minister. That night Glory House was
packed. It was my first time to meet Jess.

I was sitting next to Apostle Jim Mihlhauser when Jess prophesied very
accurate words to him which included the important role that he played
as my spiritual mentor. Then Jess prophesied to me and said, "The Lord is
showing me a picture of you doing a music festival and being all over TV—
not for your benefit but to glorify God." He went on to speak other accurate
things that only God knew about me, which encouraged me, strengthened
me, and confirmed that I was following God's voice.

This prophetic word helped me make adjustments that aligned my will with God's which now included picking back up the Austin United Music Festival that I thought was dead. Later, when the fullness of time came, the TV ministry prophecy also came to pass.

During the rest of 2005 and into 2006, I dug deeper into learning all that I could and I began practicing the use of spiritual gifts through workshop-type settings at ministries like Glory House. Various prophets, traveling through Glory House, confirmed the apostolic calling upon my life as did Prophet Michial Ratliff who I met once during a divine appointment that took place at a home church.

At first, I didn't have a clue how to walk out a godly vision. God had rewarded my obedience for praying in tongues at Church Under the Bridge by leading me into experiencing Five-fold ministry. Apostle Jim Mihlhauser gave me wise counsel, became a sounding board, and helped me stand when tremendous spiritual warfare came at me. Jim also helped me to avoid the pitfalls of religious traps that tried to prevent the free-flowing movement of God's Holy Spirit.

The spiritual gift of prophecy confirmed my calling. God equipped me with spiritual gifts to strengthen me so that I would have the courage to grab hold of the vision which God had birthed. My only question now was how in the world do I walk out a vision, since the only thing I knew for sure, at this point, was that I didn't have a clue.

Turns out, that was my best qualification.

Scripture References

This letter is from Paul, an apostle. I was not appointed
by any group of people or any human authority, but by Jesus Christ himself
and by God the Father, who raised Jesus from the dead.
(Galatians 1:1)

This letter is from Paul, chosen by the will of God
to be an apostle of Christ Jesus, and from our brother Timothy.
(2 Corinthians 1:1)

Dear brothers and sisters, I want you to understand
that the gospel message I preach is not based on mere human reasoning.
(Galatians 1:11)

Do not stifle the Holy Spirit. Do not scoff at prophecies,
but test everything that is said. Hold on to what is good.
(1 Thessalonians 5:19–21)

May God equip you with all you need for doing his will. May he produce in you,
through the power of Jesus Christ, every good thing that is pleasing to him.
(Hebrews 13:21)

Now these are the gifts Christ gave to the church: the apostles,
the prophets, the evangelists, and the pastors and teachers.
Their responsibility is to equip God's people to do his work
and build up the church, the body of Christ.
This will continue until we all come to such unity in our faith
and knowledge of God's Son that we will be mature in the Lord,
measuring up to the full and complete standard of Christ.
Then we will no longer be immature like children.
We won't be tossed and blown about by every wind of new teaching.
We will not be influenced when people try to trick us with lies so clever they
sound like the truth. Instead, we will speak the truth in love, growing in every
way more and more like Christ, who is the head of his body, the church.
He makes the whole body fit together perfectly.
As each part does its own special work, it helps the other parts grow,
so that the whole body is healthy and growing and full of love.
(Ephesians 4:11–16)

Self-Reflection Questions

Am I stepping out in faith to exercise spiritual gifts?

Do I have a spiritual father or spiritual mother who holds me accountable and mentors me?

Am I walking out my faith journey in relationship with other godly men or godly women?

Do I listen to others who try to help me by speaking correction into my life?

Meditate on the scripture verses in this chapter.
How do they apply to my life?

Chapter 24

The Beginning of Unity

Jesus responded,
"Didn't I tell you that you would see God's glory if you believe?"
~ John 11:40 ~

To get to this point, I had been required to make the right choices when I approached forks in the road and overcome multiple crises of belief. To continue to move forward, I had to continually take steps in the direction that I believed God's voice was leading me, seek confirmations, and make adjustments so that I could align my will to God's vision.

To recap prior events, the Lord led me to the Crow Nation. While hitch-hiking around the reservation, God began birthing a vision in me. After returning to Austin, the Lord led me to put together a luncheon between Austin pastors from different churches. We talked about the Walk to Emmaus and building unity throughout the Greater Austin Church Community. Out of that luncheon, a Christian music festival was birthed.

The resources came together quickly, but I walked away from people who knew what they were doing—because their vision didn't align with the vision which God was birthing inside of me. Since I did not have the know-how or resources to organize a festival on my own, I had to set the vision down and walk away. But God was clearly leading me to pick it back up again, only this time in a totally different way.

Prayer gave me the faith to come up with a new strategy, which led me back to Senior Pastors Gaylon Clark and Duane Severance. After prayerful consideration, they felt led to become part of the newly birthed Austin United Music Festival Advisory Board. Fred Thomas, who is a talented Christian musician, also joined our efforts, which brought a different perspective to our meetings.

Benjamin Anyacho set up critical meetings for me with Bishop L. A. Wilkerson and Austin Mayor Pro Tempore Danny Thomas. The Spirit of the Lord led me to other godly leaders who also became members of the advisory board.

Two huge confirmations reassured me that God was directing the steps that I took towards the vision which was unfolding. After Benjamin Anyacho set up critical meetings for me to meet with Bishop L. A. Wilkerson, we realized that it was his dark SUV, with two distinct decals on the back bumper, that gave me my personal escort to my baptism at Remembrance Gardens on July 2nd, 2003. The second was when Mayor Pro Tempore Danny Thomas agreed to host our meetings at Austin City Hall, which to the best of my knowledge is the only time a Christian organization ever held meetings like that at Austin City Hall.

The Austin United Music Festival started coming together nicely and then I received word that a very powerful religious leader wanted to meet with me. I was hoping that he would throw the full weight of his political support behind me, but instead, he told me that he didn't think that someone like me was qualified to lead something that important. He also told me that Church Under the Bridge wasn't a church and that I should go back to being a member of Gateway Church.

Though I didn't know it at the time, he would do everything he could to stop my efforts from that point on. He even called members of the advisory board to persuade them to resign and some did. In spite of his discouragement, and all the obstacles that he placed in my path, Apostle Jim Mihlhauser encouraged me to remain obedient to what God called me to do. Because my relationship was centered on Christ, He gave me the strength to keep moving forward.

I would not even mention the trials I faced except that I want you to understand that but by the grace of God, I would never have succeeded. This particular trial taught me the necessity of a fatherly covering in remaining faithful both to God and His call.

I will never forget driving to our first Advisory Board meeting at City Hall and what happened there. On my way, the devil jumped all over my thoughts and filled my mind with fear. It was so intense that I was tempted to turn my car around and go home. Satan spoke suggestive thoughts into my mind disguised as common sense, by saying, "What do you think you are doing? You can't chair a meeting with these spiritual giants who preach every Sunday. They will chew you up and spit you out." I quieted the storm by declaring out loud, "For I can do everything through Christ, who gives me strength" (See Philippians 4:13).

In our first meeting, I shared the pieces of the vision that I knew. It was tense until Mayor Pro Tempore Danny Thomas stepped forward and broke through the atmosphere by saying, "I've prayed about this. God is with this young man, so I am totally in." After that, one by one, everyone else agreed. Later, political pressure caused some to change their minds. Since Danny was on board and never wavered, we were able to secure the privileged rights to host the festival at one of the most sought-after locations in the heart of downtown Austin; Auditorium Shores at Town Lake.

During our meetings, I kept waiting for the Advisory Board to offer resources for the festival, but they didn't. God had moved me from Gateway Church to serve with Pastor Duane's homeless ministry, which didn't even have people resources much less funding. I realized later this would be for His glory, so I would not look to Gateway Church for funding but to God. Then a board member said, "It looks like this group is done meeting unless God confirms us moving forward by providing the resources." Then, for the second time, it appeared that the Austin United Music Festival was dead.

God's favor opened door after door, but I found myself being confronted again and again by the same old religious spirit that had crucified the Old Testament prophets and kept the Pharisees and Sadducees from recognizing the New Testament Church. Sadly, I found myself experiencing the teachings written in the Book of Nehemiah. At times, spiritual warfare attacked me from within my own camp and at other times from powerful people outside our camp.

One of the lies being spread about me was that I wasn't a man under authority. Twice, Jim Mihlhauser stood next to me when my two biggest accusers, who carried a lot of political power, made false accusations. When one of them asked Jim what it would take to get him to step out of the way, Jim said, "I don't want anything from you other than for you to let him do what God has called him to do."

While I was trying to be faithful in walking out the vision, and barely holding on, word reached my ears that the Senior Pastor of Great Hills Baptist Church was trying to raise three million dollars to bring Franklin Graham's organization to Austin to do a huge evangelistic crusade. After I heard that news, I once again pulled the blinds shut in my condo, curled up in a fetal position, and asked God to take away the burden that He placed on me to organize the unity festival. Instead, God told me not to worry about what they are doing and to keep focused on what He asked me to do. I found out later that Franklin Graham didn't feel comfortable coming to Austin, because they didn't have the support from Austin's minority community. Most of my advisory board was from the minority community including Mayor Pro Tempore Danny Thomas.

One day while praying, God told me to call each and every member of the Advisory Board and tell them that I had lost the vision for the festival and didn't know if I would ever get it back so that we could continue moving forward. Everyone with whom I spoke said they understood. I left voicemail messages for the rest.

Three days later, God's glory cloud fell on me. The Lord filled me with joy and He renewed my strength. I sat quietly and wept, saturated in God's presence (John 11:40). Then, the Lord spoke a new thought impression to me. The Lord said, "Get up. Go upstairs to your computer and type the new name of the festival." When I got upstairs, the Lord said, "Rename it The Power of the Cross Festival." Afterward, I called each member of the Advisory Board and told them that God had told me to keep moving forward and that the Lord renamed the festival "The Power of the Cross Festival."

Scripture References

They demanded,
"By what authority are you doing all these things?
Who gave you the right to do them?"
(Mark 11:28)

Then the Lord said to me,
"Write my answer plainly on tablets,
so that a runner can carry the correct message to others."
(Habakkuk 2:2)

I was not appointed by any group of people or any human authority,
but by Jesus Christ himself and by God the Father.
(Galatians 1:1)

Now all glory to God, who is able,
through his mighty power at work within us,
to accomplish infinitely more than we might ask or think.
(Ephesians 3:20)

Self-Reflection Questions

Am I experiencing God who rewards those who seek Him diligently?

Do I see God at work in, around, and through my life's journey?

Am I making the right choices when I come to forks in the road?

What does the "Power of the Cross" mean to me?

How does it apply to my life?

Meditate on the scripture verses in this chapter.
How do they apply to my life?

Chapter 25

The Power of the Cross Festival 2006

AUSTIN AMERICAN-STATESMAN
October 16th, 2006
"Praying for a Musical Miracle—Christian Festival Organizer Seeks to Unite Churches, Inspire City by Eileen E. Flynn
James Butt believes that 40,000 people will attend Saturday's Power of the Cross Festival at Auditorium Shores. He spent $100,000 of his own money to create the free Christian musical festival, which will feature 27 local Christian bands on three stages. "God wants to bring the full body together," he said. As Butt understands it, that means bridging denominational and racial divides.'"

Around this same time, I received a phone call from reporter Eileen Flynn that breathed new life back into the nostrils of the festival. She said that the *Austin American-Statesman* would like to interview me now that they had discovered that I was producing the first-ever Christian music festival at Auditorium Shores. After she wrote two very nice articles, I had massive amounts of people coming at me from every different angle but I didn't have a clue how to figure out who I could trust.

After the first article came out, it seemed like every Austin musician came crawling out of the woodwork to tell me that had God told them that they were supposed to perform at the festival. I also received calls from people who wanted to volunteer. When I felt led, I took people who had special skill sets to lunch so that I could form an executive leadership team. Suddenly, I had the manpower that we needed to move the vision forward from the spiritual birthing stage.

The Greater Austin Church Community began taking notice. Soon I found myself sitting at a conference table with LifeAustin Church's Senior Pastor Randy Phillips of Phillips, Craig, and Dean. Also at the table was Riverbend Church's highly respected worship composer, Carlton Dillard. A high-level representative from the biggest local Christian music station, currently called Spirit 105.9, was also there.

The radio station's representative told me they would like to help organize the festival but only under certain preset conditions; giving the station exclusive rights to promote the festival, selecting all the headline bands themselves, and running a ton of promotions. I was also told that I needed to limit the festival to one stage instead of three. After prayerful consideration, I turned down their generous offer, because their vision was different from what God had given me. He wanted me to build a festival in a way that would promote greater unity among the Austin community of believers.

Executive team members Pat Trochta, Scott McCoy, Pari Rossi, Daniel R. Garza, Cheryl Flagmeier, Mike Markley, Andrew Mabry and other highly qualified servant leaders helped me because we all felt led to be a part of what God was orchestrating; something greater than had ever been attempted before. During our leadership meetings, we found ourselves facing all kinds of unknown variables but the biggest was wondering if the churches would support our efforts. Since our goal was to bring together all the churches, para-church ministries, and governmental agencies that serve our city, we were brought to our knees, where we belonged, but especially me. At our meetings, they kept asking, "What are you doing that is attracting intense spiritual warfare and causing such a big political ruckus?"

We began by creating a database of over 300 churches. Back then, one didn't exist. Later, our list was used by various organizations to build bridges connecting Austin churches. We also created a targeted list of every para-church ministry that we could find. To encourage greater participation, we offered everyone free booth space. When the church didn't come forward to fund the festival, I cashed in all of my 401(k), IRAs, and other retirement savings to pay for the festival. We hoped this would increase participation. It didn't. Instead, word got back to me that rumors were spreading that I was wasting money which could be better spent in other ways.

Since Austin has so many great Christian musicians, we decided to make the first festival a local event which we hoped would draw church participation. Then we decided to engage the entire capacity of Auditorium Shores so we could squeeze in three stages and twenty-seven different bands. We also felt like we needed to offer a grand finale. Thankfully, worship conductor Cody Holley stepped forward to help us showcase Austin's amazing Christian talent.

The Austin Convention & Visitors Bureau assisted our efforts because by charter they are required to assist publicizing major events at Auditorium Shores. One day, I received a call from a staff member wondering if I had the support from all the University of Texas Christian organizations. Although UT's 50,000 student population was certainly a key target, I informed them that we had been blocked from getting their participation. The staff member told me that he would have it brought up the next day at the campus-wide board meeting for Christian organizations.

He called me back a few days later and told me that the festival was brought up but then a very powerful person killed the discussion by saying, "No. We won't be supporting that event." He went on to tell me, "That was it. His comment ended the discussion." Since we couldn't get support from UT Campus Ministries, executive team member Cheryl Flagmeier went to San Marcos and recruited help from Texas State Christian Campus Ministries who filled all the open volunteer positions. Praise God!

One morning Barry Brooks called me to ask if I thought about filming the music festival. My initial response was, "No, I haven't. I am overwhelmed working full-time on everything else that is involved in putting together this festival." Barry went on to tell me that Omega Broadcast would probably film the event for free if I asked, since owner David Fry was a very solid Christian. He gave me David's number and I agreed to pray about calling him.

After I felt led to call David a few days later, he agreed to provide the equipment that we needed to film the main stage provided that I supplied all the volunteers needed to man eight video camera positions for ten hours of filming. It wasn't until after the event that I realized the spiritual significance of this last-minute addition. This fulfilled the prophetic word spoken over me months earlier at Glory House by Prophet Jess Bielby who said, "The Lord says you will be all over TV, not for your glory but to glorify God."

The first *Austin American-Statesman* article created great word-of-mouth buzz which was critically important since we had a tiny advertising budget and no headline bands. Lots of people started talking about our event.

Then, one month before our festival, the Rolling Stones announced that they would be coming to Austin, for the first time ever, the day after our event. They also announced that they were limiting the attendance to seventy thousand people. From that point on, all anyone talked about was the Rolling Stones who were building the biggest stage that anyone in Austin had ever seen for their October 22nd, 2006 Festival.

The second *Austin America-Statesman* article, the one shown at the beginning of this chapter, was appropriately named, "Praying for a Miracle." From a worldly perspective, we knew we didn't have the advertising budget, headline bands, or other components which are normally needed to attract record size crowds, but we had lots of faith.

Executive team member Daniel R. Garza was in charge of selecting the twenty-seven local Christian bands that performed at the festival. When the bands showed up, he gave each member a sticker for their shirt which read, "Performing for an Audience of One." After the festival, I thought a lot about the wisdom that led him to create that, because I was too focused on the way that the world defines success which is by the number of people who show up.

The executive team members did an amazing job. Twenty-seven bands performed on October 21, 2006. They played their hearts out in the heart of downtown Austin. Unfortunately, most of the church didn't show up to support what was supposed to be a united effort.

When the festival was over, I felt heartbroken. Once again, things hadn't worked the way that I had perceived they would, only this time my pocket-book was wiped out—including my retirement savings.

The Valley of Crucified Thoughts is the place where God takes our world and turns it upside down so that He can teach us what right side up really looks like. It is the place where God breaks apart mental strongholds by placing us in positions that make us reexamine everything we think we know about God and what we believe we understand about ourselves.

I wondered, "What did I do wrong and what could I have done differently?" I also wondered why Jesus allowed politically powerful Christians to treat me so badly and sabotage the festival.

Then, while camped out in the Valley of Crucified Thoughts, I realized that Jesus didn't say we wouldn't experience persecution or being wrongly accused. Quite the opposite. Jesus said, "Since they persecuted me, naturally they will persecute you. And if they had listened to me, they would listen to you." (John 15:21). "But James, I thought you said there were *two* Power of the Cross Festivals?"

We'll get to that.

For now, let me end this chapter by sharing that I have grown and matured through opportunities like this one which have taught me a great deal about the birthing of a godly vision, working with others, character development, spiritual warfare, and the importance of treating other Christians with extra grace, forgiveness, and respect since the enemy is always at work sowing division.

Scripture References

God blesses you when people mock you and persecute you
and lie about you and say all sorts of evil things against you
because you are my followers.
Be happy about it! Be very glad!
For a great reward awaits you in heaven.
And remember,
the ancient prophets were persecuted in the same way.
(Matthew 5:11–12)

We can rejoice, too,
when we run into problems and trials,
for we know that they help us develop endurance.
And endurance develops strength of character,
and character strengthens our confident hope of salvation.
And this hope will not lead to disappointment.
For we know how dearly God loves us,
because he has given us the Holy Spirit
to fill our hearts with his love.
(Romans 5:3–5)

Stay alert!
Watch out for your great enemy, the devil.
He prowls around like a roaring lion,
looking for someone to devour.
(1 Peter 5:8)

Self-Reflection Questions

Do I believe that God can work miracles through my life?

Am I willing to share the Gospel, knowing that to do so will attract persecution?

What is God challenging me to do that benefits His Kingdom purposes?

Does my lifestyle reflect the life of those who were in Jesus' inner circle?

In the face of challenges and difficulties, do I stay faithful?

Meditate on the scripture verses in this chapter.
How do they apply to my life?

Chapter 26

Producer at Austin Public Access Television

May you experience the love of Christ, though it is too great to understand fully. Then you will be made complete with all the fullness of life and power that comes from God. Now all glory to God, who is able, through his mighty power at work within us, to accomplish infinitely more than we might ask or think.
~ Ephesians 3:19–20 ~

While recuperating emotionally from the 2006 festival, David Fry called me from Omega Broadcasting. David said, "We shot ten hours of video footage. When do you want to pick up the tapes?" While preparing for the festival, I never once thought about what would happen after the festival. I asked David to tell me what I needed to do to get the tapes shown on TV. He said, "First, you need to get an editor. Then you need to find an Austin public television producer so that you can broadcast the footage on Austin Public Access TV."

I looked up video editors and called a few. Most wanted between $150 and $350 per hour. I was told it could take up to five hours to edit each hour of footage. Since I didn't have an extra twelve grand sitting around to spend on video editing, I began praying about what to do. While praying, I remembered the prophetic word that God had spoken through Prophet Jess Bielby before the festival which was, "You are going to be all over TV but not for your glory but to glorify God." I still didn't know what that meant, but it gave me the courage to look into taking editing classes at Austin Public Access TV.

When I went to the station, I found out that I had to become a producer in order to get the tapes played, so I rolled up my sleeves and became a student. They offered classes on everything that I needed to learn; editing, lighting, sound, camera, and any other course requirements for mini-studio and main-studio certification.

While I was getting certified, I met Jonathan Mayberry at a Christian event that I produced. After helping him complete his studio courses, we were able to start producing two weekly TV series. One day Jonathan told me that the scheduler told him that we had reserved the mini-studio for three hours on Sunday. After telling me he didn't reserve it, he asked if we needed it before he canceled it. "Yes, we do," I told him. I explained that I had felt led to launch a third series called *New Life, Powerful Testimonies*, which was based on Revelation 12:7–11. Then I asked him if he knew anyone with a great personal testimony. Jonathan said he was sure he could find some people, so we agreed to keep the studio time.

I received a phone call the next morning from a publicist in Philadelphia. She asked if I was the producer of the Cross Festival. When I told her yes, she told me that she was calling to find out if I would like to book Chris Plekenpol to speak at the next festival. She shared that Chris had graduated from West Point, served in Iraq, and had written a number of books including *Faith in the Fog of War*. The publicist also told me that Chris was traveling around the country promoting his book at various TV and radio stations and that currently, he was in Florida. When I asked where he was from, she told me Dallas. (He is now the lead pastor at Wells Branch Community Church in Austin, Texas.)

Suddenly, I realized that God was at work setting up a divine appointment with Chris' publicist. I asked her if Chris would be available to come down to Austin on Sunday so that we could tape his personal testimony. She called Chris, who prayed about it, then she called me back to let me know that Chris felt led to come to Austin, and would bring three people who also had amazing personal testimonies to share.

The lobby was packed when I arrived at the station, so I took everyone into the producer's lounge to explain the procedures we would use. I began by telling everyone the name of the new series and then I stopped talking. The Holy Spirit made me keenly aware of the person standing next to me, on my immediate right. I looked him straight in the eye and asked, "Who are you?" He said, "My name is John Cochran and I am here to do whatever you need me to do." I laughed, saying, "I need another producer to get this new series on TV."

John asked me what it would take for him to become a TV producer. I told him, half-jokingly, that he would need to become a full-time student and take all kinds of certification classes quickly. To my surprise, he said, "If my commercial real estate partner will cover for me, I'll do it." Just like that, I had my third producer who also became my strongest ministry partner.

I worked, without any support or compensation, fifty hours a week recording, editing, and producing Christian content on Austin Public Access TV. The first project I edited was the Cross Festival tapes. When I completed them, I figured out how to repackage the footage a million different ways to meet programming requirements to fill up all the open time slots the station had with fresh new content.

New Life, Powerful Testimonies really took off after Pastor Paul Ojeda from Austin Powerhouse Church invited me to speak to his congregation. After I shared with them what we were doing, members of his congregation came down to the TV studio so that we could record their personal testimonies which I plastered all over the airways. This helped Paul's church grow. I did the same thing with the Cross Festival tapes. I sliced, rearranged, and repackaged the tapes in a million different ways that mixed together their powerful personal testimonies with footage from the Cross Festival.

God's Spirit attracted additional volunteers who enabled us to start producing live Christian music events in the main studio at Austin Public Access TV. Around this time, I received a call from the Austin Parks and Recreation Department telling me that I needed to put down another deposit to secure Auditorium Shores. Until then, I didn't know that I had first right of refusal locked in to rebook the highly sought-after music festival location. John and I began praying about doing another festival and received the confirmation we had been asking for, so I made the deposit.

The TV station loved the fresh new content which they desperately needed after a change in management. After God connected me to another person who became a producer, I became the executive producer of five weekly Christian TV shows—something which had never been done by anyone at Austin Public Access TV. God's grace was the anchor for my soul which enabled me to stand.

The TV shows enabled us to support the church, para-churches, and Christian musicians who came on our shows. The shows uplifted our spirits, bridged the gap between what would turn out to be two festivals, and strengthened the 501(c)(3) that I created called United in His Love which I thought would help legitimize our efforts since I still wasn't receiving any support from churches. The shows also provided an opportunity for our volunteers to develop career skills to support themselves and other ministries. I continued to serve church and para-church ministries that couldn't afford to hire videographers.

We estimated that United in His Love created over 500 hours of Christian programming, distributed over three public TV channels throughout Austin. Other Christian organizations saw what we were doing and they followed in our footsteps to take advantage of the resources offered through Austin Public Access TV. Up until we started doing what God called us to do, most of their programming was secular including *The Atheist Experience* which aired at the same time as one of our shows on another channel.

Scripture References

For I am about to do something new.
See, I have already begun! Do you not see it?
(Isaiah 43:19)

I know all the things you do,
and I have opened a door for you that no one can close.
You have little strength,
yet you obeyed my word and did not deny me.
(Revelation 3:8)

So, my dear brothers and sisters,
be strong and immovable.
Always work enthusiastically for the LORD,
for you know that nothing you do for the LORD is ever useless.
(1 Corinthians 15:58)

For we are God's masterpiece.
He has created us anew in Christ Jesus,
so we can do the good things he planned for us long ago.
(Ephesians 2:10)

Work hard to show the results of your salvation,
obeying God with deep reverence and fear.
For God is working in you,
giving you the desire and the power to do what pleases him.
(Philippians 2:12–13)

Now all glory to God, who is able,
through his mighty power at work within us,
to accomplish infinitely more than we might ask or think.
(Ephesians 3:20)

Self-Reflection Questions

What does the "fullness of life" mean?

How does that term apply to my life?

Do I believe that God can and wants to do amazing things through my life?

What kinds of adjustments do I need to make to experience the fullness of life?

Am I seeing God at work around me, and am I accepting His invitation to partner with Him?

Meditate on the scripture verses in this chapter.
How do they apply to my life?

Chapter 27

The Power of the Cross Festival 2007

*Then he said to the crowd, "If any of you wants to be my follower,
you must give up your own way, take up your cross daily, and follow me.
If you try to hang on to your life, you will lose it.
But if you give up your life for my sake, you will save it.
~ Luke 9:23–24 ~*

The TV ministry was fun, exciting, and great things were happening! One day while in the studio, I received a phone call from a web developer who ended up creating one of the most amazing festival web sites that I've ever seen. It featured a cross being raised up automatically when people opened the home page. I spent about $10,000 on the site from my personal savings, but it was worth it because the web site helped us attract great up-and-coming Christian bands, including some from across the Midwest.

We auditioned some bands live on our TV shows, and rented a video production truck to record the artists playing at the second festival. Untitled, Epic Rescue, Kingsfall, Distal, Maria Long, Devin Garza, Sylvester Treadway, and Jon the Revalaytor performed. The Fred Thomas Band not only headlined our event, but Fred also set up free sleeping accommodations for all the out-of-town bands at a brand-new condominium community, which was hugely generous.

The same politically powerful person, who was the biggest obstacle to the first festival, tried to prevent the second festival from taking place, too. He called Paul Ojeda, from Austin Powerhouse Church, and tried to persuade him to withdraw his offer to provide the volunteers that we needed to staff the second festival. When Paul took me to lunch the next day, he told me that he could hardly sleep because he tossed and turned all night long. Then Paul told me that God told him that He would double the size of his church if he ignored the opposition and kept his commitment to provide the volunteers that we needed. Today Bishop Paul Ojeda has one of the larger churches in Austin, Texas, and he is recognized as a city leader.

Since I didn't receive support from the Greater Austin area churches, John Cochran and I pretty much drained our personal bank accounts to fund the second Power of the Cross Festival. Jess Bielby, from Wichita, Kansas, arranged for a semi-truck load of food, worth about $55,000, to be delivered to Austin which we distributed freely during the festival.

The devil, full of deceit and the father of lies, perverted the truth and planted a computer expert in our camp. Initially, he tricked me. He pretended to be a helpful servant, but deviously defrauded us of the email databases that we had worked so hard to create and used it against us. It was not until after the second festival that I found out that he had sent emails to all the pastors telling them lies about me that discouraged them from participating. I didn't realize it then, but when I look back at my Judas experience, I am grateful to be counted worthy to experience this type of persecution since difficult lessons like these accelerated my spiritual growth.

I forgave Judas, who betrayed my trust, and others who might have wronged me over the years, realizing that the devil is the one who divides the brotherhood. In hindsight, I realize that my motives weren't always pure, and I didn't always treat people who co-labored with me the way that I should have while I gained spiritual maturity.

During the first festival, Daniel Garza made sure that all the musicians knew that our goal was this: Please an Audience of One. When musicians contacted me about the second festival, I made sure that each band prayed about whether or not God was truly calling them to travel here on a mission trip to perform.

It's hard to get people to show up to a free Christian event when the weather is bad. It rained off and on throughout the day. While it was happening, my heart broke and shattered into a million pieces. I felt horrible for the bands like Untitled who traveled all the way from Chicago to perform. To make matters even worse, I learned that one of their vans broke down on their way home.

If we defined the festival from an attendance perspective, the festival was a total flop. When it was over, I crawled back into the Valley of Crucified Thoughts. Once again I found myself questioning everything I thought I knew about God and everything that I thought I understood about my own Christian walk. My soul searched for quick answers, but few answers came. It wasn't until much later while traveling down the narrow path that few find and fewer follow that God gave me answers. This helped me to see things from a higher level of spiritual maturity.

After the first festival, I thought I understood what it meant to be committed to pleasing an audience of One. Truthfully, I was still worried about winning approval and pleasing people. I still looked at things from a worldly perspective; the view from the front side of the cross. Unfortunately, it's the only side the vast majority of people ever see.

Anyone can say they are committed to serving God. The questions haunting me after the second festival were, "Did I really mean it?" and if so, "Would I be willing to do anything, including having my heart broken again, to follow Jesus?" Like the deer frozen in the headlights, I found myself staring at a new sign in the middle of a new fork in the road. This time the sign read "Total Reckless Abandon."

Suddenly, a new proposal divided my soul and spirit which judged the thoughts and attitudes of my heart. Was I ready to become Christ's bond-servant? Or would I follow in the footsteps of Jesus' disciples who turned back while saying, "This teaching is too difficult." (See John 6:66).

Scripture References

The message of the cross is foolish
to those who are headed for destruction!
But we who are being saved know it is the very power of God.
(1 Corinthians 1:18)

Our lives are a Christ-like fragrance rising up to God.
But this fragrance is perceived differently by those who are
being saved and by those who are perishing.
(2 Corinthians 2:15)

"But I, the Lord, search all hearts and examine secret motives.
I give all people their due rewards,
according to what their actions deserve."
(Jeremiah 17:10)

Obviously, I'm not trying to win the approval of people, but of God.
If pleasing people were my goal,
I would not be Christ's servant.
(Galatians 1:10)

At this point many of his disciples turned away and deserted him.
Then Jesus turned to the Twelve and asked,
"Are you also going to leave?"
(John 6:66–67)

Live a life filled with love, following the example of Christ.
He loved us and offered himself as a sacrifice for us,
a pleasing aroma to God.
(Ephesians 5:2)

Self-Reflection Questions

Am I willing to pick up my cross daily and follow Jesus?

What does it mean to deny myself, go anywhere, and do anything?

What did Jesus mean when he said, "those that lose their life will save it?"

How does "The Power of the Cross" apply to living missionally for Christ?

Meditate on the scripture verses in this chapter.
How do they apply to my life?

Chapter 28

Total Reckless Abandon

At about three o'clock, Jesus called out with a loud voice,
"Eli, Eli, lema sabachthani?" which means
"My God, my God, why have you abandoned me?"
~ Matthew 27:46 ~

While traveling down the narrow road that few follow, I found myself lost at what appeared to be a dead end. I was finally broke. This time my savings, stocks, retirement, and other funds were completely gone. The funny thing about thinking you are financially broke is there are usually other avenues that you haven't thought about which you can tap into, but this time I really was flat broke. I had to sell my car so that I could buy food and continue to make the mortgage payments on my condo. When that money ran out, I started making the payments using my credit card. I really was flat broke!

One day, Jess Bielby called to check up on me. When I updated him on my situation, he asked if I had any equity in my condo. When I told him that I did, he shocked me when he told me to sell it while I could still get my equity back. He helped me realize that the bank would take everything if I didn't do something quickly. Until he called, my mindset was frozen in the belief that God would somehow rescue me since I had been faithful by sowing everything that I owned since giving my life to Christ five years earlier. Although I didn't understand it back then, I was trying to hold tightly to the things I thought would satisfy my soul rather than allowing Jesus to pour a new foundation for my life which filled it with meaning and purpose.

When I asked Jess what I should do after selling my condo, he suggested that I prayerfully consider buying his 1978 Winnebago Chieftain and strapping a used motorcycle to the back of it so that I would have an inexpensive way to get around to sightsee. He said he would sell me his thirty-one-foot motor home for $6,500. Jess said, "Go have fun and enjoy yourself until your money runs out. When it does, God will tell you what to do next." Suddenly, I was facing another *crisis of belief*, only this time it was selling my condo, getting rid of all my possessions, and traveling out West until I spent everything that I had left. Since I was also emotionally spent, I felt like I had come to the absolute end of myself. Like the biblical story of Jonah and the whale, I can relate to Jonah saying, "Just pick me up and throw me into the stormy sea." I give up. I am done. I surrender!

I contacted Jeanne Butterfield, the agent I bought the condo from. I told her that I needed to sell right away and that I didn't want someone tying up the contract and backing out. A father ended up purchasing it for his daughter because he wanted her to live in a safe community. Jeanne told me she saw him praying and then he said, "Yes, this is the one for sure. We will take it and this contract will go through." I took this for another confirmation. We closed on it right before the stock market crashed in 2008.

After signing the contract, I had thirty days to get my affairs in order before we closed so I could head out West. The first thing I did was set up a United in His Love board meeting with Barclay Garman, John Cochran, and Rod Ladd. Since Rod said he felt led to take over the nonprofit, he signed the paperwork and then I gave him everything that I had been managing, including the $10,000 worth of video equipment that I had purchased from my personal funds to do all the video editing for our TV shows. I then sent emails to all 300 pastors in our database to inform them that I was stepping down from United in His Love. I encouraged them to support Rod since I would no longer be involved. Out of all the emails I sent out, I only received one back. It was from Bishop Kenneth Phillip, at PromiseLand Central Church, who said he was sorry to see me going.

While leaving Austin, the orphan spirit of total rejection was heavy on me. My heart was broken. My mind, will, and emotions were shattered. It felt like the Greater Austin Church Community had made a ring of thorns, placed the crown around my forehead, spit in my face, chained me to a political whipping pole, and flogged me. I didn't know it then, but I was also angry at God because I felt like He had forsaken me. Later, I began to understand that everything that God had allowed me to experience had really been a blessing in disguise since everything I've experienced is part of the process of character molding and shaping which God brings us through during our souls' sanctification.

I bought a used motorcycle, loaded it into the back of a U-Haul, drove it to Kansas and picked up the RV from Jess. Then I drove out West and saw things most Americans only dream about finding the time to see, during the trip of my lifetime.

During the next three months, I put thousands of miles on the RV and 14,000 miles on the motorcycle, riding through the scenic byways in

Colorado, Utah, Arizona, and California. The trip's highlights included US National Parks: Zion, Bryce Canyon, Arches, Lake Powell, Antelope Canyon, Monument Valley, and Yosemite. Another highlight was driving up the Pacific Coast Highway in California.

Jess called me while I was in California. He said he was bringing together a Five-fold ministry team to start a church in Springfield, Missouri. He invited me to be a part of it. I had just enough gas money to drive the RV from California to Missouri. Then, when I reached New Mexico, the RV broke down again for the umpteenth time. The problem this time was that I didn't have funds to fix it and neither did Jess, who suggested I call someone else for help.

When I called my mother, she said she didn't have any money to give me. I then called my second ex-wife, Terri, who said she would think about it and told me to call her back the next day. After I did, she told me that she had been receiving quarterly statements from a stock fund that was still in my name even though it was part of my divorce settlement. She told me that they had been sending her statements for the past five years. (If I had known about it, I would have cashed it in earlier to contribute more towards the festivals which means I wouldn't have had it available then.) Suddenly, I had the funds I needed to fix the RV and fund my living expenses for the next six months.

It's amazing how God works things out that are above and beyond all we can think or even imagine.

Scripture References

The helpless put their trust in you.
You defend the orphans.
(Psalm 10:14)

And everyone who has given up houses . . . or property,
for my sake, will receive a hundred times as much in return
and will inherit eternal life.
(Matthew 19:29)

Unless the Lᴏʀᴅ builds a house,
the work of the builders is wasted.
(Psalm 127:1)

And we know that God causes everything to work together
for the good of those who love God
and are called according to his purpose.
(Romans 8:28)

And this same God who takes care of me
will supply all your needs
from his glorious riches,
which have been given to us in Christ Jesus.
(Philippians 4:19)

So let's not get tired of doing what is good.
At just the right time we will reap a harvest
of blessing if we don't give up.
(Galatians 6:9)

Together with Christ we are heirs of God's glory.
But if we are to share his glory,
we must also share his suffering.
(Romans 8:17)

Self-Reflection Questions

Do I really know God as intimately as I should?

Am I traveling down the narrow path that very few find?

Have I truly entered into a deep and intimate relationship with Jesus?

What does "forsaking all, so that I might gain Christ" look like in my life?

Meditate on the scripture verses in this chapter.
How do they apply to my life?

The Ministry
of Reconciliation

Chapter 29

A Place to Rest My Head

We can rejoice, when we run into problems and trials,
for we know that they help us develop endurance.
And endurance develops character,
and character strengthens our confident hope of salvation.
And this hope will not lead to disappointment.
For we know how dearly God loves us,
because he has given us the Holy Spirit to fill our hearts with his love.
~ Romans 5:3–5 ~

After having spent three months traveling out West, I felt refreshed when I arrived in Ozark, Missouri, a little town just south of Springfield. I remember enjoying the leaves changing color that fall of 2007 and was excited about being part of planting a new church and what I thought would be a career as an ordained minister under Gospel Associates, Jess' ministry organization. I looked forward to meeting and being a part of a Five-fold ministry team that flowed in spiritual gifts so that we could equip others for greater works.

I was looking forward to fulfilling the calling God had on my life which had been prophesied over me many times. What none of us knew was that God didn't bring us together to start a church, but instead to crucify our flesh while preparing us for other assignments.

The church didn't plant after six months, and Kevin Goodwin ended up moving to Honduras, which is where he continues to head up an orphan adoption ministry. Will Deeds moved down to Guatemala to serve as a missionary before moving back to Kansas to serve as a Senior Pastor, and others have ended up serving in different ministries in other capacities.

When the dust settled, I found myself stranded in Missouri, separated from everyone that I knew. With nowhere to go and very little money, I began praying. Then God directed my attention towards a picture of a low-income housing facility in Springfield, Missouri. Then the Lord said, "I want you to go there now. Don't think about it. Get in your van and go now."

I grabbed my keys, jumped in my van, and started driving towards Springfield, a 20-minute drive. (I had given the RV back to Jess, at which point I was given a van.) While driving, I got ahead of myself. I assumed that God was finally going to let me get back to having a normal job making money again and that I would be renting a room at this low-income housing facility, that used to be a one-hundred room hospital.

When I called ahead to the Franciscan Villa Apartments, the first person I talked to asked me if I had a job. When I told her that I believed that God was putting me back to work, she didn't seem to care. She told me that I didn't qualify to move in there. Then she said the only way you could qualify to move in here is through one of their two transitional housing rooms, both of which were filled with a waiting list to get in. I replied, "I am a man of faith. I believe I am supposed to be moving in there, so I am heading your way to learn more."

I hung up my cell phone and found myself facing another *crisis of belief*. I was tempted to turn around and drive back to Ozark but tried to remember exactly what I thought I clearly heard God say. The Lord had said, "Don't think about it. Get in your van and go there now."

Suddenly, I realized God didn't tell me to phone ahead. By now, I wasn't sure what I believed, but I had just enough faith to drive the rest of the way there so that I could at least see if God was really setting me up with a divine appointment.

It wasn't until I arrived that I discovered that the person to whom I had previously spoken was the assistant manager. She introduced me to Teresa, who was the manager in charge. Teresa asked me to fill out a transitional housing application and then she said, "You never know."

Three days later, while I was praying, the Lord said, "You need to contact Teresa. She is supposed to do something." That is all I heard. I wasn't sure what that meant so I sent Teresa an email which said, "Teresa, I am writing to you because you said you're a Christian. I need to ask you to pray about something. The Lord told me to tell you that you're supposed to do something, but I don't know what that is. God just told me to ask you to pray." Three hours later, Teresa called to offer me a job as a night security officer in exchange for one of the transitional housing rooms that had suddenly become available.

I had gone from being a white-collar guy used to making six figures to working two nights a week as a night security guard in exchange for a room, three hot meals a day in the basement kitchen, and living in a low-income housing facility. Needless to say, this wasn't what I expected when I moved to Missouri to help start a church.

While praying during the third morning after I moved into the apartment, I had "A Come to Jesus Meeting" with myself. I cried out to God, complaining like a little child that didn't get his way. I reminded God that I had been faithful and that I had given Him everything that I owned. Then, while on my knees, I said, "God, is this where I am supposed to be? Have I lost my mind? I can't take this anymore. Please put me out of my misery and just kill me." After I finished complaining, I found myself facing another *crisis of belief*, only this time it was wondering whether or not I was where God wanted me to be.

Then God answered my prayer by saying, "Get up. Call Teresa. Tell her that I asked you to start teaching Bible studies." I called Teresa. When she picked up the phone, I said, "Teresa, the Lord told me to start teaching Bible studies here. You lead and I'll follow." I didn't know why I said it that way and neither did she. Teresa said, "Ok, James, whatever you say." Click. She hung up on me.

The next morning a couple of widows walked into Teresa's office and told her that they wanted to start a Bible study, but they didn't know anyone who could teach. They wondered if she could recommend someone. Teresa called me and said, "James, I wasn't sure what to think about your phone call yesterday. Can you come down to the office? You're supposed to meet some people."

I needed to know that I was exactly where God wanted me to be, and the Bible study confirmed it. Later that day, I received a second confirmation after I went to my bank. That is when I learned that I only had $50 left to my name. I had spent the entire amount that I had received from cashing in the stock fund that I had discovered after my RV broke down.

Scripture References

"My thoughts are nothing like your thoughts," says the Lord.
"And my ways are far beyond anything you could imagine."
(Isaiah 55:8)

And this same God who takes care of me
will supply all your needs from his glorious riches,
which have been given to us in Christ Jesus.
(Philippians 4:19)

These things dominate the thoughts of unbelievers,
but your heavenly Father already knows all your needs.
(Matthew 6:32)

Don't be like them,
for your Father knows exactly what you need
even before you ask him!
(Matthew 6:8)

This Good News tells us how God makes us right in his sight.
This is accomplished from start to finish by faith.
As the Scriptures say,
"It is through faith that a righteous person has life."
(Romans 1:17)

Self-Reflection Questions

Have I stepped out in faith to allow God to develop my spiritual character?

Am I committed to being in a totally committed relationship with Jesus?

If the world ends tomorrow, am I ready to meet my Creator?

Do my possessions possess me?

Am I willing to let go of my possessions to follow Jesus anywhere?

Meditate on the scripture verses in this chapter.
How do they apply to my life?

Chapter 30

Blooming Where God Plants You

God has given each of you gifts from his great variety of spiritual gifts.
Use them well to serve others.
~ 1 Peter 4:10 ~

After moving into the Franciscan Villa Apartments, I started teaching Bible studies and discipling some of the widows who lived there. One woman, who was in poor health, died suddenly. When her relatives came into town, they asked Teresa if she knew a pastor that would be willing to conduct the woman's funeral service. Teresa called me and asked, "James, can you come down to the office? You're supposed to meet some people."

I agreed to do the service after the family agreed to allow me to use it as an evangelical opportunity to lead others to Christ. Teresa placed invitations in all the residents' mailboxes. At least half of them attended the services that we held in the old hospital sanctuary which still served as a chapel. Suddenly, I had a captive audience who had come to celebrate her life which also proved to be the perfect opportunity for God to establish my ministry. God also led the granddaughter of the deceased and others to come forward during the glorious altar call. Praise the Lord!

That Sunday, I invited a few of the people that I was discipling to attend services with me at Dayspring Church. While we were there, we filled out visitor cards which triggered Dayspring's Outreach Team to do visitations where we lived. While talking to a few people that I was discipling, Pastor Paul Smith, Kristi, and Rance discovered that I was actively doing ministry so they came to my apartment to meet me and asked if they could come alongside the work the Lord was establishing through me.

I was thrilled to be aligned with others that had a heart for outreach. Their visit also led to me becoming firmly planted at Dayspring Church which became like family. I got involved as much as I could which included serving in the food pantry, creating a promotional video for the church, and washing dishes after dinner was served to the Celebrate Recovery participants.

The Lord connected me to three people who were a huge blessing to me while I lived in Springfield; Pastor Farley Lewis, who asked me to be part of his home visitation team operating in the gifts of the spirit; Brent Smallwood, who invited me to be part of his team which moved powerfully in the prophetic to evangelize and strengthen God's church; and Christa, who became my strongest ministry partner. Together we pushed the boundaries of our faith through evangelism, prophecy, healing, and outreach ministry.

Where I lived was the perfect place to do ministry because it was filled with people suffering from addictions and mental disabilities. We also did street evangelism. Sometimes others would join us, but most of the time, it was just Christa and me experiencing God's administration of grace working through spiritual gifts like words of knowledge, discernment of spirits, healing, and very accurate prophetic words.

One day while I was ministering to a young woman, the Lord told me to ask her if "firecracker" meant anything to her. Startled, she looked at me and asked, "How did you know that my parents called me that while I was growing up?" After getting her attention, the Lord spoke additional words of knowledge through us to minister powerfully to her which brought tears to her eyes. These kinds of experiences became common.

The Lord also worked powerfully through Brent, who carries a special anointing to bring prophetic people together to minister to others. Once, Brent invited me to a large Baptist church gathering for singles at Wendell Lovewell's home. After almost everyone left, Brent said that he believed the Lord wanted those of us who remained to pray for Wendell.

I sensed God's presence, which set up the situation. When Brent began speaking, we automatically came into agreement which confirmed the Lord's presence. Suddenly, accurate prophetic words started flowing through Brent, Christa, and Becky. Then the Lord spoke through me, saying, "The Lord is showing me a vision of a gift. I see your hands unwrapping the paper of a gift with strings around it and a bow. The Lord wants you to know that tonight He is giving you the gift of discernment." After everyone was done prophesying, Wendell told us that the spoken words were very accurate and shared how two nights before, his intercessor felt led to come to his house and pray that God would give him the gift of discernment to help him manage the large groups of people that would be showing up at his house. Then Becky, Brent, and I prayed and Wendell received the baptism of the Holy Spirit and the gift of speaking in tongues. Weeks later, he opened up his home to Five-fold ministry gatherings.

During the years that I lived in Springfield, I worked as a night security guard in exchange for room and board. (No money changed hands.) I still needed money to do things like pay for car insurance, gas, razors, shampoo, and other essentials. I will be eternally grateful for Brent, Christa, and the others who sowed love offerings into the work the Lord did through me while I lived there. Through them, I learned to trust the Lord's faithfulness!

Scripture References

For we are God's masterpiece.
He has created us anew in Christ Jesus,
so we can do the good things he planned for us long ago.
(Ephesians 2:10)

A spiritual gift is given to each of us so we can help each other.
To one person the Spirit gives the ability to give wise advice;
to another the same Spirit gives a message of special knowledge.
The same Spirit gives great faith to another,
and to someone else the one Spirit gives the gift of healing.
He gives one person the power to perform miracles,
and another the ability to prophesy.
(1 Corinthians 12:7–10)

Jesus came and told his disciples,
"I have been given all authority in heaven and on earth.
Therefore, go and make disciples of all the nations,
baptizing them in the name of the
Father and the Son and the Holy Spirit.
Teach these new disciples to obey all the commands I have given you.
And be sure of this: I am with you always, even to the end of the age."
(Matthew 28:18–20)

Self-Reflection Questions

Am I blooming where God plants me?

Am I developing a lifestyle of servanthood?

Am I using the gifts God has given me to serve others?

What's keeping me from being totally committed to serving Christ?

Am I fulfilling the calling that Jesus placed on my life?

Meditate on the scripture verses in this chapter.
How do they apply to my life?

Chapter 31

God Heals Two Women

Jesus called his twelve disciples together and gave them authority
to cast out evil spirits and to heal every kind of disease and illness.
~ Matthew 10:1 ~

One morning, I found myself having a pity party about being a night watch-
man and being stuck in Springfield. In the midst of my complaining, the Lord
told me to get dressed and go prayer walking. During the entire time that I lived
in Springfield, I never went on a prayer walk by myself so this was definitely
something new and extraordinary. For those of you who have not experienced
this, prayer walking is when we step forward in faith, making ourselves avail-
able so that God's will can be done on earth, through us, as we become Christ's
hands, feet, and voice.

I grabbed my iPod, laced up my sneakers, cranked up the praise music, and
began walking. While worshiping, I prayed for God to arrange divine appointments. During the first fifteen minutes of brisk walking, I didn't walk
by anyone. Suddenly, three little puppies were biting at my ankles. Then I
noticed someone on my right, who appeared to be saying something, so I
turned off my iPod. She said, "Don't move or they will keep following you.
I'll come to you."

While the woman walked towards me, I intensified my prayer. I prayed that
she was a divine appointment. When the woman reached me, she thanked
me for not moving. I looked at her and BOLDLY said, "I am prayer walking. How can I pray for you?" She told me she didn't need prayer because
everyone in her family is a believer. I surprised both of us when I looked at
her again and said BOLDLY, a second time, "I am prayer walking. How can
I pray for you?" Juggling her puppies, she turned around and said, "Follow
me." Then she walked inside her home leaving the door wide open. While
continuing to pray, I stopped when I reached the threshold.

My concern about being alone with a woman in her house went away
when I looked into the house and saw the woman's husband sitting on the

couch talking on the phone. I walked through the living room and followed her into the formal dining room that also had a desk with a computer located in the corner. The woman told her daughter, who was doing something on the computer, to get up. Then she said, "God sent this man to come here and pray for you." The husband stood up saying that he wanted to be included. Since something supernatural appeared to be happening, I asked, "What's going on?" They told me the day before two different doctors told them that their daughter had cancer.

The four of us got in a circle, grabbed hands, and then they started praying. I sensed they were from an old-school, black Pentecostal church. While they were declaring and decreeing, and shouting all kinds of things, I silently prayed, asking God what He wanted me to pray. Then, I placed my hand on her and said a simple prayer. When I did, I experienced a unique thought impression telling me that God just healed her. It was so strong I felt led to write down their contact information so that I could come back and document the healing.

When I left their home, I continued prayer walking. Ten minutes later I came across an elderly man polishing his car. We both had our eye on each other. While I walked towards him, I prayed for it to be a divine appointment. When I finally reached him, I said, "I am prayer walking. How can I pray for you?" He looked at me and while smiling said, "I don't need you to pray for me. God already healed me. I have a daughter just like you who brought some friends with her to pray for me. God healed me of cancer." His testimony was a confirmation that God had healed the young woman whom I prayed for minutes earlier.

Christa called me one day six months later to partner together to do ministry. The game plan that day was to walk around Walmart looking for people who were disabled or limping, or to spot other such divine appointments. After she picked me up, I asked her to make a quick stop to document the healing that had taken place at the young woman's home who had been diagnosed with cancer. While heading to the address, we stopped at a garage sale which was a half-block from where we were heading.

While Christa was looking around, the Lord gave me a word of knowledge or thought impression that the garage sale was a divine appointment. Then I noticed that besides the couple holding the garage sale and their two kids, no one else was around except Christa and me. It was if we were encapsulated in a unique moment, separated from any distractions.

I asked the man and his wife why they were having the garage sale. They told me that he was a Baptist pastor in between jobs and they were getting ready to move. Then the Lord encouraged me to share testimonies about supernatural healings to build their faith. Suddenly, I found myself having to overcome another *crisis of belief* since I knew that some Baptists don't believe that spiritual gifts are still active in today's church.

By now Christa had noticed that I had engaged in conversation, so she stopped looking around and joined in. I shared some amazing stories which included the young woman we were going to see and other healings which we had witnessed God doing. Then the woman said, "We prayed for someone who got healed once. For a month they stayed healed and then the illness came back. Then we did a Bible study about the Holy Spirit which taught us that the spiritual gifts mentioned in the book of Acts are no longer active."

While the woman was speaking, the Lord gave a word of knowledge to Christa. Then Christa said to the woman, "You have a woman's issue that has to do with your blood, don't you? You need healing yourself, don't you?" Startled, the woman looked towards her husband to get his permission, and then she turned back towards Christa and said, "Yes, I do. Because of the blood issue, we had to adopt our children."

Christa and I looked at each other. Then Christa asked the pastor's wife if she would allow us to lay hands on her and pray for God to heal her. The woman looked at her husband again, who nodded his approval. After we prayed, Christa asked her how she would know if God had healed her. The woman beamed, saying, "I already know that God just healed me." Christa asked, "How do you know?" The woman said, "While you were praying for me, my sinuses cleared up, my headache went away, and all the other symptoms, which I've always had, disappeared! I know God just healed me!"

Suddenly, the Baptist pastor, who had been very reserved up until this point, leaped out of his chair asking us to pray for him. I asked him why he needed prayer. He told us that he had hepatitis. After we placed hands on him and prayed, we believed that God healed him because hepatitis is asymptomatic.

We left the pastor's home and drove up the street to where the young woman with cancer lived. Christa and I knocked on the door, and the mother answered. She told us that at her daughter's checkup that took place after my prior visit, the doctors couldn't find any cancer. Praise the Lord!

Scripture References

Jesus called his twelve disciples together and gave them authority
to cast out evil spirits and to heal every kind of disease and illness.
(Matthew 10:1)

A woman in the crowd had suffered for twelve years
with constant bleeding, and she could find no cure.
Coming up behind Jesus, she touched the fringe of his robe.
Immediately, the bleeding stopped.
(Luke 8:43–44)

For the Father loves the Son and shows him everything he is doing.
In fact, the Father will show him how to do
even greater works than healing this man.
Then you will truly be astonished.
(John 5:20)

I tell you the truth, anyone who believes in me
will do the same works I have done.
(John 14:12)

These miraculous signs will accompany those who believe:
They will cast out demons in my name,
and they will speak in new languages.
They will be able to place their hands on the sick,
and they will be healed.
(Mark 16:17–18)

Confess your sins to each other and pray
for each other so that you may be healed.
The earnest prayer of a righteous person has great power
and produces wonderful results.
(James 5:16)

Self-Reflection Questions

Do I believe that Jesus still does miracles on earth through His disciples?

Am I living a self-centered life, or am I a conduit for God's Kingdom?

Do I believe in the power of prayer that activates supernatural grace?

When was the last time I prayed for someone else?

Why don't I do it more often?

Meditate on the scripture verses in this chapter.
How do they apply to my life?

Chapter 32

Four Divine Appointments – Easter 2009

My message and my preaching were very plain.
Rather than using clever and persuasive speeches,
I relied only on the power of the Holy Spirit.
I did this so you would trust not in human wisdom, but in the power of God.
~ 1 Corinthians 2:4–5 ~

I will never forget what happened while driving to Dayspring Church on Easter Sunday. A cold front had blown in the night before making the weather miserable. As I approached Kearney Avenue, I saw a man walking in the cold rain. While driving past him I noticed that he was carrying his belongings and that he wasn't wearing any rain gear, so I pulled my van over ahead of him and turned it around to position it directly in his path.

I figured I would invite the man to attend church with me so that he could at least get out of the bad weather for a while. When he got close enough, I rolled down my window and began to speak. I started to say, "Would you . . ." The man, who was really demon-possessed, screeched a satanic hissing kind of sound that made the hair on the back of my neck stand up. Then I noticed his very scary face. Suddenly, I found myself facing another *crisis of belief.* Though I was frightened, prayer enabled me to become willing to confront the demon, but God didn't give me the unction to chase after him or do anything other than pray for his soul and become aware of what just happened.

The whole experience was very troubling. I found myself confused which led me to pray harder for answers. For the life of me, I couldn't figure out why God would allow me to experience something like that without giving me the faith, power, and inspiration to do something about it. Finally, I just threw my hands up in the air and prayed, "God, I am confused. If you want me to cast out demons or serve you in some other way, then you are going to have to make your will clear. If you want me to give someone a ride, you'll need to make it more obvious. If you want me to pray for someone, then you need to give me the courage, wisdom, power, inspiration, and opportunity to do it."

After church, I drove back to the Franciscan Villa Apartments using a different route. I was getting ready to turn from Chestnut onto Main, which is four blocks from Scott Street, where the apartments are located when I noticed another man walking in the rain, but he was wearing a nice leather jacket. My mind quickly recalled the demonic being that I tried to help before church. I looked but the man didn't signal that he needed a ride, so I kept driving towards my apartment while reminding the Lord of my prayer before church. For some reason, I still felt guilty that I didn't stop, so I prayerfully reminded the Lord that I would serve Him but only if He took the guesswork out of trying to figure out His will.

I parked my van and walked through the basement passageway and into the residents' kitchen. After grabbing some food at the buffet, I sat down. When I looked up, in walked the guy in the leather jacket. Then to my surprise, he walked directly to our table where I was sitting with three other people (instead of any of the other thirty-nine tables) and asked the guy next to me if he could give him a ride home. Clearly, God was at work in front of me and I was being invited to join God's plan. The kitchen isn't easy to get to, hardly anyone except residents ate there, and I had never seen this guy before. God clearly orchestrated what was unfolding which also called my bluff about being willing to help if God made His will known. Without any hesitation, I spoke up and said, "I'll give you a ride. Let me finish eating and I'll take you home."

We talked during the long drive to where he lived, which was across town. He told me he was married and that he hadn't gone home the night before. Not only did he cheat on his wife, but he also admitted that he had a drinking and drug problem. Then, the Lord ministered very powerfully to him through my personal testimony. Before he got out of my van he had repented of his sins, promised that he and his wife would get help, and asked Christ into his life. While driving back to my apartment, I patted myself on the back and gloated while praying; "See, God, that wasn't so hard. If You make Your will known, things will work so much easier for both of us."

As I turned into the Franciscan Villa parking lot to get ready for my security guard shift, a woman jumped in front of my van. She climbed into the passenger seat before I could figure out what was happening. When I looked at her, God said, "I had this one wave at you, didn't I? She is a prostitute. I want you to minister to her and tell her that I love her." The woman asked me to give her a ride to her sister's house. While driving, we talked about her life, my personal testimony, her getting help at Victory Mission, God's love, and the power of prayer. When we arrived at her sister's, she broke down in tears while we prayed. Then with a big smile on her face, she got out of my car and walked into the house.

This time, while driving back to my apartment, I didn't gloat and kept my mouth shut. As I was reporting for my shift, Richard Schultz, a resident I had been discipling, appeared and informed me that he was ready to accept Christ into his life. We found a quiet room and got down on our knees to pray. Richard repented from the practice of witchcraft and sorcery and asked Jesus Christ to make a home in his heart. A few weeks later, he came with me to Dayspring Church to get baptized. Praise the Lord!

A few months later, Richard mentioned that he had a very strange encounter while walking to the convenience store; he was hissed at by a demon-possessed guy who was perched in a tree. After Richard's encounter, I remembered that the Bible tells us that we never know when we are entertaining angels that appear as humans. I believe we also come across people who are under the influence of demons.

Scripture References

This letter is from Paul,
a slave of God and an apostle of Jesus Christ.
I have been sent to proclaim faith to those
God has chosen and to teach them
to know the truth that shows them how to live godly lives.
(Titus 1:1)

When we tell you these things,
we do not use words that come from human wisdom.
Instead, we speak words given to us by the Spirit,
using the Spirit's words to explain spiritual truths.
(1 Corinthians 2:13)

Each time he said, "My grace is all you need.
My power works best in weakness."
So now I am glad to boast about my weaknesses,
so that the power of Christ can work through me.
(2 Corinthians 12:9)

Self-Reflection Questions

Is my faith just a religion or is it real and experiential?

Am I experiencing God working in and through my life consistently?

Do I hear God speaking to me, and what is He trying to tell me?

Is my faith based on my intellect and willpower, or on God's grace?

Meditate on the scripture verses in this chapter.
How do they apply to my life?

The Father's Provision

Chapter 33

Supernatural Grace

God confirmed the message by giving signs and wonders
and various miracles and gifts of the Holy Spirit whenever he chose.
~ Hebrews 2:4 ~

While living in Springfield, I held onto the hope that was wrapped around a prophetic word prophesied over me before I sold my condo in 2008. The prophet, who didn't know anything about me, said, "God is showing me a vision of you doing a lot of traveling, ending up somewhere for a few years, and then another prophet, who loves God dearly, bringing you back to Austin. Like Barnabas to Saul, this man will reintroduce you to the Austin church."

One day, in 2010, while praying, God told me he wanted me to give away my white van. My knee-jerk reaction was hesitation since my first thought was that I needed the van to get back to Austin someday. After overcoming my initial *crisis of belief*, I called Associate Pastor Farley Lewis at Dayspring Church. I told him that God told me to give away my van. That Sunday, after church, I handed Farley the keys. Two weeks later, Farley informed me that the church's mechanic looked at the van and they decided they didn't want it. I was quite surprised that they didn't accept my love offering, so I prayed. When I did, I realized God didn't tell me who to give the van to.

In prayer the following day, I remembered David, who heads up a homeless ministry, told me a year earlier they could use a van like mine, so I decided to approach him. When I asked if he still needed a van, David said, "No, I don't need a van, we need a truck." After trying to give the van away twice, I told God, "I must have heard wrong. If you want me to give the van away, you are going to have to make it super obvious and give me multiple confirmations, because I am done trying to give this van away."

During this time frame, the Lord was doing some amazing things through me prophetically. I volunteered to bag groceries at Dayspring's amazing food pantry ministry. One day the woman who led the food pantry ministry came up to me while I was bagging groceries and told me she believed that I was supposed to join her team to pray for the next person who was coming into the prayer room. That was the only time she ever asked me to join her prayer team. When the man entered the room, he sat next to me. The prayer leader asked me, "Has God given you something to pray for him?" While praying silently for a prophetic word, God didn't give me anything. So she asked the man, "What do you need us to pray for you?" He said, "I need a van. Mine broke down and I need another one. It doesn't need to be new. A used van is all I need." I nearly fell off my chair, but remained silent and prayed to God for more confirmations.

Three days later, while walking to Dayspring, I was praying again about the van. Suddenly, the same man I had met at the food pantry crossed the street in front of me and walked into his house, which showed me where he lived. That night, God gave me peace about this being the right person, so the next morning, I drove to the man's house and signed over the title. Although I didn't realize it then, giving away the van as a love offering set into motion the fulfillment of God's prophetic word spoken years before.

Charlie Lujan, from PromiseLand Church in Austin, contacted me a few weeks later to inform me that Bishop Phillips wanted to talk to me. Although I didn't have a personal relationship with the Bishop, he told me God had illuminated me to him in his prayers so he wanted to discuss bringing me back to Austin to be part of PromiseLand Church. Soon after our phone call, I was called into the Franciscan Villa Apartments office. The new manager, who had replaced Teresa, informed me that they were interviewing people for my job as a night security guard. I was told that I would have to move out as soon as they found my replacement.

A few days later, Barclay Garman, one of the final board members of United in His Love, contacted me, independent of the Bishop's call, and said that he felt led to send me $2,000 so I could buy a car. Within days of Barclay's call, John Cochran, of the same board, called to inform me that he and his family felt led to invite me to live with them at Point Venture, Texas, a second home community on a lake outside Austin. He said, "We have a spare bedroom and enough food to feed you until God re-establishes your finances."

Clearly, God was closing doors and opening new ones. At this point, I didn't have any options other than following the path which God was clearly orchestrating. So, I packed up, drove to Texas, and moved in with the Cochran family. I was still some distance from PromiseLand Church and lacked the gas money to keep driving the hour there and back again. A few months later, Linda Chandler, who pastors the Austin Brethren Church, contacted me. She said she felt led to pay for the monthly rental and utility fees which enabled me to move into an apartment for six months in Austin.

Now that I lived fairly close to PromiseLand Church, I started getting more involved. I led a very strong soul winning action team (SWAT) that included Mary McLin, Francis Boafo, Iris Tsosie, and Christella Calvo and her sister Delia. Others from various churches joined our efforts because they saw God moving through us in a miraculous way. We went door-to-door at apartment complexes leading people to Christ and videotaping their personal testimonies, which I uploaded onto YouTube. Suddenly, all kinds of people started joining our weekly efforts. This created a training issue, so we put together an evangelistic training seminar.

During this time I was also creating promotional videos for various PromiseLand Ministries. One day while helping Ed Mancias, a lady who had moved here from Russia overheard me telling him that my apartment arrangement with Pastor Linda Chandler was ending and that it looked like I might be homeless in another week. Upon hearing this, she offered to allow me to live rent-free in a very nice home that had recently become available in Jester Farms, a nice neighborhood just north of Austin in Round Rock.

After praying about it, and facing the possibility of being homeless, God told me that her kind offer wasn't for me, so I posted about it on Facebook which led to Rick Claeson to contact me about a German missionary couple and their three teenage kids who needed a place to stay. Since I already knew them, I introduced them to the Russian lady who was happy to offer them her home.

While everything was unfolding, Barclay Garman invited me to live with him until I got back on my feet. Soon after, Brad Roberts and I became Facebook friends, and Brad moved in with us. Like Barclay, he was also going through a divorce. Since I had already been through what they were experiencing, I helped them while God was re-establishing me in Austin.

Scripture References

For I have appeared to you to appoint
you as my servant and witness.
Tell people that you have seen me,
and tell them what I will show you in the future.
(Acts 26:16)

We are witnesses of these things and so is the Holy Spirit,
who is given by God to those who obey him.
(Acts 5:32)

Focus on reading the Scriptures to the church,
encouraging the believers, and teaching them.
Do not neglect the spiritual gift you received
through the prophecy spoken over you
when the elders of the church laid their hands on you.
Give your complete attention to these matters.
Throw yourself into your tasks so that everyone will see your progress.
(1 Timothy 4:13–15)

God blesses those who patiently endure testing and temptation.
Afterward they will receive the crown of life
that God has promised to those who love him.
(James 1:12)

Self-Reflection Questions

Am I seeing God's fingerprints on the activities that surround my life?

Do I see signs, wonders, and miracles occurring consistently?

Am I walking in humility, or am I too full of pride, thinking that I cannot learn from the giftings of God that flow through others?

List times where pride has hindered me from growing in my walk with God.

List times where pride has hindered me from learning from others.

Are all my treasures stored up on earth, or have I made deposits in heaven?

Meditate on the scripture verses in this chapter. How do they apply to my life?

Chapter 34

A Head-on Collision with Destiny

And this same God who takes care of me will supply all your needs
from his glorious riches, which have been given to us in Christ Jesus.
~ Philippians 4:19 ~

One day, Barclay came into my bedroom and told me sternly that it was time
for me to get a real job or else I needed to find another place to live. Then he
really motivated me when he said, "Humble yourself, if need be, and apply at the
convenience store around the corner."

I wondered about getting back into sales since I had been out of it for a
long time. Compounding my fear was the fact that I was having all kinds of
problems with the car that I was driving. But after the Lord confirmed me
getting back into sales through a prophet, I started sending out my resume
for the first time since becoming a Christian in 2003.

Around this same time, Brad asked me to give him a ride to Marble Falls
so that he could pick his truck up at a friend's mechanic shop. On the drive
back to Cedar Park, I felt a wobbling coming from the passenger's side back
wheel. I looked back over my shoulder just in time to see the back tire fly off
the car, soar fifty feet into the air in a perfect spiral, and roll down the other
side of the road into a local business. I hit the brakes and skidded across
Ranch Road 1431 towards what is normally oncoming traffic. After coming
to a stop, I drove over to the side of the road. That is when I noticed that
my car was leaning on its back axle. If another car had been coming, I could
have been involved in a head-on collision.

A few minutes later, a man appeared, shaking his fist and yelling at me
from the direction of where the tire had flown. "You almost killed me with
that tire!" Shaken, I apologized and said, "It flew off. I didn't throw it at you.
I didn't even know that a wheel could come off like that." Then I called Brad
who picked me up on his way back to Cedar Park. We had the car towed to
the nearest auto repair shop while I prayed about what to do next.

This wasn't the first time that my car had broken down. Fred Blackman and others had helped me fix it multiple times. To make matters worse, the AC had stopped working. When I tried to fix it, I was told that I needed to take it to the VW dealership since their mechanics were the only ones who could reprogram the AC computer chip. While I was driving to the dealership, the Lord brought to my attention a prophetic word that Sarah Cheikho had spoken over me while I was standing next to Christella Calvo a few months earlier. Sarah said, "God showed me a vision of you standing next to a used red Mustang convertible. In the vision, you were driving a different car than what you are driving now." Then the Lord said, "I am not going to allow you to drive this car any longer. If you fix it, it will keep breaking down. I want you to buy a car."

At that exact moment, I found myself facing a new *crisis of belief*, Melody Meserve called me. This was the first and only time that she's ever called me. While talking, I shared with Melody what God had just spoken to me. Melody said, "If God told you to buy a car, then that is what you need to do." I told Melody, "But you don't understand. I don't have a job and I am flat broke. How do you buy a car without any money?" Melody said, "Just trust God to work it out."

When I arrived at the VW Dealership, I asked the service manager where the used car lot was. He told me it was a quarter mile up the road. Leaving the VW to be repaired, I walked up the road and over to the only red Mustang convertible on the lot. It was in horrible shape so I assumed that I wasn't hearing God's voice correctly. As I turned around to walk back to the dealership, a used car salesman asked if he could help me. I replied, "I thought I was here to buy a used red Mustang, but I guess not because this car is in horrible shape." The salesman responded by saying, "Have you ever considered buying an EOS hardtop convertible?" That was a Volkswagen model. I replied, "I am sure I can't afford that." (When I used to make six figures, the old me seriously considered buying a $75,000 Lexus hardtop convertible.) The salesman replied, "You'd be surprised."

While test driving the EOS, I received a phone call from Chris Wooten. He worked nearby and said he had just finished working, so I picked him up and brought him back to the dealership with me to work out the details of buying the car. I signed what amounted to something close to a $24,000 debt. Since I didn't have any money, I ended up trading in my car in exchange for waiving the first two car payments. I knew that I would crash and burn if God didn't line me up with a job by the third month because that was when my next $349 car payment would come due. The whole time everything was unfolding Chris kept shaking his head, saying, "I can't believe you're buying this car without a job or any money." I replied, "I couldn't believe it either but all things are possible in Christ Jesus."

Weeks later, the Lord provided me with a sales job working for Knight Security Systems that came with a $700 per month car allowance which covered my car payment, insurance, and gas. I even had a little left over to cover maintenance. I didn't know it at the time, but looking back now, God had to push me outside my comfort zone to get me motivated enough to get back into sales. His purpose in taking me through this was to teach me another significant lesson.

Scripture References

God makes us right in his sight.
This is accomplished from start to finish by faith.
As the Scriptures say,
"It is through faith that a righteous person has life."
(Romans 1:17)

And God will generously provide all you need.
Then you will always have everything you need
and plenty left over to share with others.
(2 Corinthians 9:8)

May you experience the love of Christ,
though it is too great to understand fully.
Then you will be made complete with all
the fullness of life and power that comes from God.
Now all glory to God, who is able,
through his mighty power at work within us,
to accomplish infinitely more than we might ask or think.
Glory to him in the church and
in Christ Jesus through all generations forever and ever!
Amen.
(Ephesians 3:19-20)

Self-Reflection Questions

Am I my own provider, or have I entered into a God-dependent relationship?

Do I trust God, and do I really believe that Jesus can and will meet all my needs?

Have I fully grasped the riches that can only be found in Christ?

What did Jesus mean when he said, "Man doesn't live by bread alone, but by every word that God speaks into our lives?"

Meditate on the scripture verses in this chapter.
How do they apply to my life?

Chapter 35

Turns Out,
I'm No Longer a Salesman

This means that anyone who belongs to
Christ has become a new person.
The old life is gone; a new life has begun!
~ 2 Corinthians 5:17 ~

I was excited about getting back into sales when I went to work for Knight Security Systems on January 3rd, 2011. For the first time in eight years, I had a monthly paycheck coming in, medical insurance, and a one-bedroom apartment that I could afford to rent on my own.

To make a long story short, I was a horrible salesman for Knight Security System. I made one very large sale to Austin Recovery and a few small sales before Knight fired me ten months later. Although initially, I didn't understand, I soon began to realize that God was pruning my thoughts linked to my past. After I failed, I realized that the great salesman, who had broken all kinds of sales records and could sell ice to Eskimos, no longer existed.

I had wanted to get back into sales so that I could live a more normal kind of life since living by faith, up to this point, had been extremely difficult. It's hard to be in full-time ministry without any financial support or appreciation from those that you serve. It takes amazing grace, which only God can provide, to be a trailblazer focused on pleasing an audience of One.

Until I got back into sales, the biggest unsettled issue in my mind was wondering if my life would have been more fulfilling if I had gotten back into sales. The Lord knew I was struggling with that thought, which is why He allowed me to try it again. It turned out to be a trust issue all along. My concern, while walking down the narrow road that few follow, was second-guessing the below scripture references which were strategically positioned at various forks in that narrow road.

Scripture References

He cuts off every branch of mine that doesn't produce fruit,
and he prunes the branches that do bear fruit
so they will produce even more.
(John 15:2)

So don't worry about these things, saying,
"What will we eat? What will we drink? What will we wear?"
These things dominate the thoughts of unbelievers,
but your heavenly Father already knows all your needs.
Seek the Kingdom of God above all else, and live righteously,
and he will give you everything you need.
So don't worry about tomorrow,
for tomorrow will bring its own worries.
Today's trouble is enough for today.
(Matthew 6:31–34)

What's more, I am with you,
and I will protect you wherever you go.
One day I will bring you back to this land.
I will not leave you until I have finished giving you
everything I have promised you.
(Genesis 28:15)

Self-Reflection Questions

Am I living a fulfilling life? Or am I happy just trying to be 'normal'?

Is my identity tied to my work?

Who am I without a job or a title?

What lesson is God trying to teach me in this season?

Am I living to please myself, or to please an audience of One?

Meditate on the scripture verses in this chapter.
How do they apply to my life?

The Battle
To Advance
God's Kingdom

Chapter 36

The Devil Tried to Destroy Me

We were crushed and overwhelmed beyond our ability to endure,
and we thought we would never live through it.
In fact, we expected to die.
But as a result, we stopped relying on ourselves
and learned to rely only on God, who raises the dead.
And he did rescue us from mortal danger,
and he will rescue us again.
We have placed our confidence in him,
and he will continue to rescue us.
~ 2 Corinthians 1:8–10 ~

I've celebrated many holidays at the Northland Alcoholics Anonymous. The Suburban Group location is where I learned to live a sober lifestyle. I used to go back there to remind myself that my sobriety is important, to witness to new people, and to see old friends. I met my third wife at Northland on Christmas Day, 2012. While talking to a friend, a beautiful woman came bursting into the lobby, saying, "Life is good. I am having a great Christmas." The next thing I knew, she was sitting down next to me while I was eating, and she told me that she had also grown up attending the Lutheran Church occasionally with her mother. I was smitten. The previous night, I had told a friend I was content being single and living alone.

Three months later, Lucille asked me to marry her. I'd been married twice before I became a Christian. After I became a new creation in Christ, my life had so changed dramatically I truly believed that I could finally be a great husband. Lu made commitments to me too. These included allowing me to baptize her and attending church regularly. We agreed to passionately pursue Christ together.

While my wife and I began growing together, the Lord restored the finances that I had sown into the kingdom for the Power of the Cross Festivals. We went from living in a cheap apartment to inheriting enough money from my mother to buy a 1,150 square foot home located next to Hill Country Bible Church Lakeline (HCBCL) in Cedar Park, Texas. Since it came with a fenced in backyard, my wife convinced me to buy two little dogs, Cupcake and Mr. Wiggles, who to this day have blessed me tremendously with love, joy, and amazing companionship.

After careful prayer, the Lord led us to become members of HCBCL. I led a small group that met at our house on Sundays. Then the Lord connected me with Pastor Doug James and Tom Law, who oversaw HCBCL Community Impact, and with Pastor Bob Gilfillan, who headed up the benevolence ministry. One thing led to another and soon I found myself totally engaged, serving under them, doing evangelism outreach, and creating promotional videos for various outreach ministries. I also volunteered to create promotional videos for various ministries which formed the Twin Lakes Christian Compassion Resource Center.

About a year into our marriage, my wife told me that her eighteen-year-old son's best friend had committed suicide. A month later, another one of her son's friends was killed while rock climbing. Soon after that, the father of one of her son's friends died in Austin when a car ran a red light and hit his motorcycle head-on. As a result of these tragedies, Lu started spending time with her single divorced girlfriends who were mourning the deaths of their sons who had grown up together. Soon she stopped answering her phone and coming home at night. When she finally did come home, she told me she no longer wanted to be married. No matter what I said or did, there was nothing that could get her to reconsider her decision. Desperately, I reached out to everyone that might have been able to help us. But it became very clear that she had made up her mind and checked out of our marriage. After she moved out, she asked me to stop calling her.

When I got divorced for the third time, I stayed in the house because I had purchased it with money that I inherited. I also kept the two dogs since the house had a fenced in backyard. Funny how things returned full circle.

After my wife left, it felt like I had been thrown into a mixed martial arts fight with the reigning MMA heavyweight champion of this world who was determined to destroy me. Satan attacked my mind, will, and emotions. The devil whispered accusations into my ear; "I thought you were a Christian. How can a Christian get divorced? If you had been a better husband, she wouldn't have left you."

It was a terrible time. I was exhausted physically, mentally, and emotionally. I was spiritually drained. I prayed, but prayer didn't seem to help. Like Jesus while He hung on the cross, I cried out, "God, why have you forsaken me?" When God didn't answer, I curled up in a tiny little ball again and prayed for the Lord to put me out of my misery by taking my life.

I bought a used Suzuki 1200cc motorcycle so that I could take a trip to the Colorado Rocky Mountains to clear my head, think, and pray until I heard from God. Bad idea. Before I left, I sensed in my spirit that I needed to write a will that included a do not resuscitate (DNR) medical clause. Since I listed HCBCL as a beneficiary, Pastor Doug James told me to whom I needed to give a copy of my will.

The next day, I rode from Austin to New Mexico so that I could stop and visit my friend, Pari Rossi. Then I rode on to Pagosa Springs, Colorado, which is a place with many fond memories, and stayed with Pam Schoemig and her husband, Tom, at their beautiful vacation rental property. During the week I tried to relax, take great rides, clear my head, and spend time praying. I also enjoyed the hot springs at the Springs Resort & Spa.

When I left Pagosa, I rode to Ouray, Colorado and booked a hotel room for my return trip. Then I continued until I reached my destination which was to bed down that night in Montrose, Colorado. The next morning, while eating breakfast, I became friends with Jolanta Ogrodny, who owned the Western Motel with her family. Instantly, we recognized God's Spirit within each other. Before I left to go on that day's motorcycle ride, Jolanta graciously agreed to allow me to store all my gear in her office. I told her I would pick it up on my way back to Ouray.

That morning I rode the Black Canyon of the Gunnison National Park which was truly an amazing ride. While looking out from a rest area on top of the mountain, I remember thinking that it doesn't get much better than this. Then, while traveling 55 mph through Delta, Colorado, a car ran a red light and hit my motorcycle head-on.

I don't remember flying in the air or bouncing, but I do remember coming to. The first thought I had was wondering if I was still alive. The second thought was wondering if I had any paralysis. The third thought was that I needed to try and get up and get out of here before someone called an ambulance since I didn't have any medical insurance. As I began to get up, I could hear a lot of people yelling, "Stay down!" I was later told that I flew 30 feet in the air after being hit. The driver was later charged with reckless driving and driving with a suspended license.

Cody Henry witnessed the accident from his motorcycle. He took pictures and went with me to the hospital to make sure I was OK. An angel must have broken my fall because no one walks away from an accident like that one. The doctors told me I had six fractured ribs, a fractured shoulder, and a partially deflated lung. I was in extreme pain. When I was released from the hospital two days later, Jolanta picked me up. She allowed me to stay at her hotel for a reduced rate until I was well enough to fly home.

My purpose for taking a motorcycle trip to Colorado was to clear my head, think, and to pray. Instead, my trip was cut short and a miracle kept me from being killed. I needed to take the next year off in order to recover; therefore, I got to spend a lot of time alone with God, praying.

Scripture References

Stay alert! Watch out for your great enemy, the devil.
He prowls around like a roaring lion, looking for someone to devour.
Stand firm against him, and be strong in your faith.
Remember that your family of believers all over the world
is going through the same kind of suffering you are.
In his kindness God called you to share
in his eternal glory by means of Christ Jesus.
So after you have suffered a little while, he will restore, support,
and strengthen you, and he will place you on a firm foundation.
(1 Peter 5:8–10)

Timothy, my son, here are my instructions for you,
based on the prophetic words spoken about you earlier.
May they help you fight well in the Lord's battles.
Cling to your faith in Christ, and keep your conscience clear.
For some people have deliberately violated their consciences;
as a result, their faith has been shipwrecked.
(1 Timothy 1:18–19)

Each time he said, "My grace is all you need.
My power works best in weakness."
So now I am glad to boast about my weaknesses,
so that the power of Christ can work through me.
That's why I take pleasure in my weaknesses, and in the insults,
hardships, persecutions, and troubles that I suffer for Christ.
For when I am weak, then I am strong.
(2 Corinthians 12:9–10)

Self-Reflection Questions

How do I deal with disappointments in life?

When things don't go my way, will I still trust God is good?

What truths does the Bible say about my life?

Will I believe in the truths of the Bible, or the lies of the enemy?

When the enemy attack my mind, will, or emotions, do I fight back with the word and prayer?

Meditate on the scripture verses in this chapter.
How do they apply to my life?

Chapter 37

The Kingdom on Earth

During the forty days after he suffered and died,
Jesus appeared to the apostles from time to time,
and he proved to them in many ways that he was actually alive.
And he talked to them about the Kingdom of God.
~ Acts 1:3 ~

The road to recovery after my motorcycle accident took time and countless visits to Elite Chiropractic back in Austin. During those visits, Doctor Collin Hilliard and I became friends. When my lawsuit settled, I paid off the hospital bill and did videography and internet marketing work for Collin until I worked off the amount that I owed him. Afterward, he hired me to continue to help him which provided a small income which helped pay my living expenses.

When I was at my lowest point, after my third wife left, I had a conversation with a mentor that really helped. He told me that God hadn't disqualified me in any way from serving Him. He instructed me to "get back on the horse" and remain faithful to finish the race so that I can receive the prize that awaits me when Christ tells me personally, "Well done, good and faithful servant."

Over the years, I've learned that serving others is a great way to cure what ails us. One day, Rita Auerbach, who runs a non-profit ministry called Bags of Grace, asked me to create a promotional video for her ministry which serves the homeless at places like Church Under the Bridge (CUTB). Since I've created all kinds of promotional videos, over the years, to help other para-church ministries that can't afford videographers, I said yes.

While filming at CUTB, I met Todd Adams. One conversation led to another at which point I learned that Todd had been trying to find someone to go with him to evangelize the neighborhood that I lived in. After we agreed to prayer walk my community, God worked powerfully through us as ministers of reconciliation.

Throughout the summer months of 2014, I prayed a lot. I told the Lord that I was wiped out and that I couldn't afford to keep the house that I was living in because I didn't have the strength needed to hold down a normal job or the passion needed to get back in sales. I found myself telling the Lord that I would be willing to sell the house and use the equity to follow him again, but only if He made his will known. All summer long, the Lord was silent, so I kept praying, "Lord, just tell me what You want me to do, and I'll do it."

One day, at the end of the summer, I sensed that God had answered my prayer. When He did, I prayed for additional confirmations. That night Todd came over to my house. He said, "I love what God is doing through us. Every time we go out, we are leading people to Christ so I wanted to come over here and pray with you about doing this even more." I told Todd that I would do whatever God told me to do, but that I believed God just answered the prayer that I have been praying all summer long earlier that day. Then I asked Todd to pray for me so that God would give me one more confirmation on whether or not God wanted me to sell my home or continue evangelizing the neighborhood with him. The very next morning Pastor Bob Gilfillan, from HCBCL, called me out of the blue. The first words out of his mouth were, "James, are you thinking about selling your home?" I nearly fell out of my chair laughing. Then I told Bob, "I am now. Your question is the last confirmation that I needed."

I called Dow Kennedy of RE/MAX to sell my home. When I told Dow that I needed him to sell it quickly, he asked me how long I had lived in the house. When I told him I had no idea, Dow said, "Your home has appreciated a lot since you bought it. Unless you've lived in it for at least two years you're going to have to pay taxes on the increase." Then he asked me again, "How long have you lived in it?" I repeated that I had no idea. After Dow looked it up, he said, "If you sell it thirty days from today, it will be exactly two years and one day." The first couple to see my home, Randy and Janie, purchased it exactly thirty days later.

I was able to get a great deal on a new RV that was loaded with upgrades as someone had canceled their order while it was being assembled at the plant. When it arrived in Austin, weeks before I closed on my home, I needed to find a place to move it. Frantically, I called all the RV parks in Austin. Nothing was available so I started looking for places outside of Austin. I called Bastrop, Round Rock, Elgin, Georgetown, and RV parks further out. Nothing was available anywhere.

Suddenly, I found myself facing another *crisis of belief*. My first thought was, "Did God really tell me to sell my home?" Quickly, I recalled that I did have three very strong confirmations. Then, I began trying to recall why I felt led to purchase the RV. Since those confirmations weren't as obvious, I got down on my knees and cried out to God. In a loud voice I said, "Lord, I told You that I was willing to sell the house and follow You. I believed You led me to buy the fifth wheel. Did I make a mistake? Lord, I am confused. Jesus, I need Your help. Show me what to do. I need Your help." When I finished praying, I got up off my knees, sat down in front of my computer and did a new Google search—"RV park near Lake Travis, Texas." Soon I found a truly amazing place on the lake called Camper Resort Lake Travis.

When I called them, someone named Chuck answered the phone. After grilling me, he agreed to an interview. When I arrived at the RV park, Chuck asked me what seemed like a million different questions along the lines of, "Why should we allow you in?" (Exactly one year later, I found myself representing Christ as I stood at his death bed asking him the same question: "If you die, why should Christ allow you into heaven?")

As Chuck continued to grill me, I wondered whether or not I would be permitted to move into the RV park. Then his wife, Mary Ellen, joined us. Finally, Chuck threw up his hands in the air and asked, "Just tell me this. Why do you want to move in here, and where are you living now? My response was, "I am selling my home, and have bought a brand-new fifth wheel which I need to move right away." Chuck responded, "We have a couple living here in a fifth wheel that is buying a home in Cedar Park." I told Chuck, "I am selling a home in Cedar Park." Then Chuck said, "We found out last night that they are buying a home on Mulberry Way." Laughing, I said, "I am selling a home on Mulberry Way."

Mary Ellen chimed in, "Their fifth wheel is only fifty feet from here. I am texting them now to tell them to come down here quickly." As Randy and Janie Fox approached us, Chuck asked them, "Do you know this person?" They looked at me and both said, "No." Then Chuck asked, "Are you buying his house?" Suddenly, Janie, Randy, and the rest of us started laughing. Clearly, God was at work doing something among us. One hour later, they welcomed me to move into the RV park. We became friends, and they introduced me to the rest of the Small Acts RV Community.

After moving in, a neighbor came down to my fifth wheel to introduce herself. Carolyn Parson said, "I heard you're a pastor and that you knew Pastor Duane Severance." I said, "Yes, he was a dear brother. I am grateful that the Lord prompted him to call me the day before he passed away so that we could talk one last time." After we talked for a while, she asked if I would be willing to serve as a volunteer pastor, like Duane did, at Lake Travis Crisis Ministry. I said I would be honored to since her invitation was a strong confirmation that I was exactly where God wanted me to be.

The master was full of praise.
"Well done, my good and faithful servant.
You have been faithful in handling this small amount,
so now I will give you many more responsibilities.
Let's celebrate together!"
(Matthew 25:21)

She told them that Jesus was alive and she had seen him,
they didn't believe her.
Afterward he appeared
in a different form to two of his followers.
They rushed back to tell the others, but no one believed them.
Still later he appeared to the eleven disciples
as they were eating together.
He rebuked them for their stubborn unbelief
because they refused to believe those who had seen him
after he had been raised from the dead.
And then he told them,
"Go into all the world and preach the Good News to everyone.
Anyone who believes and is baptized will be saved..."
And the disciples went everywhere and preached,
and the LORD worked through them,
confirming what they said by many miraculous signs.
(Mark 16:11–16, 20)

Self-Reflection Questions

What *crises of belief* (tests of faith) am I facing?

Am I willing to take risks to overcome *crises of belief?*

Do I believe in a miracle-working God?

Will I trust God for a miracle by asking Him?

Meditate on the scripture verses in this chapter.
How do they apply to my life?

Chapter 38

Building the Kingdom

The LORD ordered that those who preach the Good News
should be supported by those who benefit from it.
Yet I have never used any of these rights.
And I am not writing this to suggest that I want to start now.
I would rather die than lose my right to
boast about preaching without charge.
~ 1 Corinthians 9:14–15 ~

While settling into RV living, I began serving at Lake Travis Crisis Ministries. As I was waiting for the Lord to tell me what He wanted me to do next, I spent time alone with Jesus; praying, reading daily devotions, meditating on scriptures, mentoring others, discipling people through Facebook, and listening to Christian worship music, which kept me centered throughout the day.

One day while praying, the Spirit led me to contact Chuck Stevens. Afterward, Jess Bielby asked me to set up a prophetic ministry meeting at Chuck's home church. Weeks later, another prophet from Salado contacted me to set up a meeting with Jess at another home church that called themselves "The Watering Well."

At those gatherings, we were all ministered to prophetically. Three different prophets confirmed the calling that God has on my life and prophesied that God wanted me to write this book. I then received a fourth confirmation from another prophet who had friended me on Facebook. Knowing that the Lord had ordained the time and place for me to write gave me the strength I needed to begin what turned out to be a monumental task.

There are many common threads interwoven throughout my story of the narrow path that few find and even fewer follow. While reflecting on God's administration of grace, I am also reminded that God's timing is always perfect. It's never early but is always exactly on time.

The 2016 central Texas Memorial Day flood set records which totally filled Lake Travis and flooded the RV lots located below us. The rising waters threatened the rest of us living at Camper Resort, Lake Travis.

While praying about hiring someone to move my fifth wheel into storage, I received a phone call from Laura Berndt who encouraged me to pray about going on a short-term mission trip to South Dakota. She serves in God's kingdom by ministering and serving Lakota Sioux First Nations People on the reservations, of which there are a total of 9 in South Dakota. What I thought would be a week-long trip turned into more than a month! God had other plans and I had the privilege of serving on both the Cheyenne River and Standing Rock Reservations.

During the drive to South Dakota, I stopped in Kansas to see Jess Bielby, who had ordained me. The Lord had placed it upon my heart to ask Jess to confirm my authority to ordain others, and by God's grace, I was given permission to ordain whomever the Lord chose, and freedom to oversee those whom I ordained.

There at the home office, I asked if I could ordain Laura under Jess' 501(3) (c) since she works full-time serving different ministries and is a helpful partner in editing my books. Laura has never received compensation from any ministry she has served and has never been publicly recognized for her selfless efforts.

Upon my arrival in South Dakota, I stayed with Laura's family and served with her in and around Mobridge and on the reservations. I observed how hard she labored, the challenges she faced, and her unwavering dedication. While serving with Laura, I met other pastors from various denominations.

I sought confirmation from others concerning what I was hearing in the spirit realm concerning Laura's ordination. Not only did the other pastors agree, but all of them wanted to participate in her ceremony. It was a glorious event. (If you recall, Laura gave me my first Bible and the book *Experiencing God* by Henry Blackaby.) Happily, God had placed me in a unique position to participate in what He did to honor her. Praise God!

While serving in South Dakota, Laura lined up opportunities for me to share my testimony at several churches, including a church pastored by Donna Archambault, a member of the Standing Rock Sioux Tribe. The Lord revealed insight as to what He was doing in and through Donna during a service, which I released prophetically. After the service, I discovered that she not only pastored a church on the reservation but miraculously is able to produce the only Christian Radio Show called I.R.O.C.C. (an acronym for I Rely On Christ Constantly), on KLND 89.5, Little Eagle, SD. This is a secular radio station reaching Cheyenne River and Standing Rock Reservations, and surrounding areas. For twelve years she has been donating her time and talents to the Kingdom, rising before dawn every Saturday and Sunday, to go on the air from 6 a.m. to 12 noon to deliver inspirational music and scriptural messages. Donna recently said people are able to tune into I.R.O.C.C. from all over the world on the Internet, TuneIn Radio, and various other avenues. She has received messages from as far away as India and Africa!

When I asked Donna who her ordination was through, to my surprise, she said she wasn't ordained. Then she said, "I experience all kinds of spiritual warfare because people don't think I should be leading this church or hosting a Christian radio show since I'm not an ordained pastor." Like Laura, Donna had received no compensation nor recognition for her selfless efforts. It broke my heart to hear that no one had ever publicly recognized what God had clearly ordained through her, so I told her that I would be happy to ordain her. Pastors from other ministries, including Pastor Laura, participated in the ordination ceremony which took place a few weeks later at Donna's church. It was a beautiful way to acknowledge and honor her unwavering commitment to establishing Christ's kingdom on the earth.

While serving with Laura, we also finished the editorial process of the first edition of *Crisis of Belief*. Right after we uploaded it to the printer, I placed my first order for several boxes of books to be shipped directly to Nila Campbell in New Mexico. We handed them out at a tent revival that we coordinated weeks later in Aztec, New Mexico, in which many made commitments to Christ, getting baptized immediately afterward.

During the next few years, I kept in touch with Pastor Laura and Pastor Donna and shipped them several thousand dollars' worth of books to distribute freely to those they minister to. This came from the very small funds that I had which allowed this to be a blessing to their ministries. Never did I even consider asking them to tithe or sow love offerings into my ministry, since my calling is to undergird, build up, and strengthen the church.

I had an opportunity to share my testimony in Houston where I gave away boxes of free books as a discipleship tool to everyone who asked, and paid someone to build a web site to facilitate free downloads of the book for whoever wanted one.

After Houston, the Lord opened a door for me to help coordinate a seminar with Sudanese churches that met annually in Kansas City, Missouri. This created the perfect opportunity for Pastors Donna, Laura, and Jess Bielby to meet. Unfortunately, after the conference ended, Jess and I parted company over something I felt was unscriptural. We had a very sharp disagreement over something we had agreed to earlier.

Talk about a *crisis of belief*. I found myself in a situation that reminded me of the story in Acts where Paul and Barnabas had such a disagreement that they decided to part ways. For so many years, I believed I needed ordination from man to receive the recognition and funding that I needed through people who only donate to tax deductible ministries. Again, I found myself totally dependent on Christ, after being led to rip up the ordination paper that I had so desperately sought all those years. On the other hand, I was separated, like Paul and Barnabas, from one I had called a trusted brother and friend. My heart was broken, but it was clearly the leading of the Lord. We are called to peace.

The Lord reassured me that my ordination of Laura and Donna was sincere on my part. He was the one who told me that what He had already recognized in the spiritual realm concerning Laura and Donna, he wanted it to be recognized in the physical realm. All this too, was part of the testimony that the Lord called me to teach.

Jesus said, "You didn't choose me. I chose you. I appointed you to go and produce lasting fruit" (John 15:16). The apostle Paul said, "He called you to salvation when we told you the Good News; now you can share in the glory of our Lord Jesus Christ" (2 Thessalonians 2:14).

Scripture References

And we know that God causes everything
to work together for the good of those who love God
and are called according to his purpose for them.
(Romans 8:28)

The LORD says,
"I will guide you along the best pathway for your life.
I will advise you and watch over you."
(Psalm 32:8)

The LORD directs the steps of the godly.
He delights in every detail of their lives.
Though they stumble, they will never fall,
for the LORD holds them by the hand.
(Psalm 37:23–24)

You will receive power when the Holy Spirit comes upon you.
And you will be my witnesses, telling people about me everywhere
and to the ends of the earth.
(Acts 1:8)

But when the Father sends the Advocate as my representative -
that is, the Holy Spirit - he will teach you everything
and will remind you of everything I have told you.
(John 14:26)

Jesus came and told his disciples,
"I have been given all authority in heaven and on earth.
Therefore, go and make disciples of all the nations,
baptizing them in the name of the Father and the Son and the Holy Spirit.
Teach these new disciples to obey all the commands I have given you.
And be sure of this: I am with you always, even to the end of the age."
(Matthew 28:18–20)

Their disagreement was so sharp that they separated.
Barnabas took John Mark with him and sailed for Cyprus.
(Acts 15:39)

Self-Reflection Questions

Am I sowing my time, talents, and treasures into the Kingdom?

Do I demand respect, or have I learned that a true servant serves with humility?

Does my heart represent the good/fertile soil in the story of Matthew 13:1-23 that has truly accepted God's message and produces a huge harvest? Or, am I still practicing the "what's in it for me" consumption religion because the soil of my heart is hard or shallow or thorny?

Have I learned to rely on God's perfect timing and administration of grace, or am I still trying to force my will and control everything?

Meditate on the scripture verses in this chapter. How do they apply to my life?

Chapter 39

The Ministry of Reconciliation: Sharing the Good News

*Then he told me, "God chose you to know his will and to see the Righteous One
and hear him speak. For you are to be his witness,
telling everyone what you have seen and heard."*
~ Acts 22:14–15 ~

*One day, after returning home from Kansas City, I was taking a break from
writing another book and bumped into Mary Ellen, the park manager. She
asked if I knew that her husband had been sick and I told her no. Then I told her
that I would pray for Chuck. While praying, I became very concerned. I couldn't
stop thinking about the unusual look that I had seen in Mary Ellen's face while
she told me, so I asked the Lord if I should go to Chuck's RV to lay hands on him.
Since the Lord didn't answer me, I assumed that Chuck wasn't very sick.*

My neighbor Angie called me a few days later while I was with Ron and Joyce
watching the UT football game. Angie said, "I am at the hospital with Mary
Ellen. Chuck isn't doing very well. Should you be here?" I told her that I
would pray about coming. After I hung up, everyone around me started
talking about Chuck's condition. Silently I prayed, but I didn't sense that the
Lord wanted me to do anything then, so I continued watching the game.

The next morning, while praying, the Lord told me that He wanted me to
go see Chuck, but to make sure that Mary Ellen wasn't in the room. (Later
Mary Ellen explained to me why that was important.) I called Angie and
told her what the Lord told me. That is when I learned that Mary Ellen had
been sleeping in Chuck's hospital room and that she hadn't left the hospital
in two days. Angie also shared that Mary Ellen had said she planned to
come back to the RV park to take a shower sometime that day. Angie agreed
to send me a text message letting me know when it was OK for me to visit
Chuck so we could be alone.

While waiting for Angie's text message, I continued to pray. It was then the Lord told me that I needed to be in Chuck's room at exactly 3 p.m. Angie's text never came, so I went to the hospital anyway at that time. When I arrived, Angie apologized for not texting me and said Mary Ellen had just left.

When I walked into Chuck's room, he asked, "Are you staying here, too?" I responded by saying, "No. God sent me here to pray for you and talk to you about where you are going to end up spending eternity." Then I asked him about his beliefs and shared the Good News that Jesus Christ came into the world offering us the *free-will* choice of where we spend eternity. Then I asked Chuck, "Do you believe that Jesus Christ died on the cross so that your sins would be forgiven and that, through faith in Christ, rather than works, you can receive the free gift of eternal life?" Chuck said, "Yes." Then I asked, "Are you 100% certain that God will allow you into heaven?" Chuck said, "Yes."

After we settled the salvation issue, I laid hands on Chuck while praying for God to heal him. Afterward, I asked Chuck how he felt. He said, "My shoulder still hurts." So I laid hands on him a second time and prayed specifically for his shoulder. Afterward, I was told that he was sitting up doing crossword puzzles and that he was very talkative.

When I left Chuck's hospital room, Angie was waiting in the lobby. While I shared what had happened, Mary Ellen called to let Angie know that she was on her way back to the hospital. When Angie handed me the phone, Mary Ellen told me that I didn't need to hang around until she came back. I did anyway because I sensed in my spirit that I needed to tell Mary Ellen the details about what had happened while I was alone with Chuck. Mary Ellen and her son, David, broke down crying. That is when I learned Mary Ellen and other believers had been praying for Chuck's soul for years because they were worried about where he would end up spending eternity.

A few days later, I started receiving group text messages from our community saying that Chuck's health was deteriorating rapidly. After getting down on my hands and knees, my heart broke into a million pieces as Christ's compassion fell upon me. While weeping in God's overwhelming presence, I asked the Lord if He wanted me to go and lay hands on Chuck again. The Lord said, "Wait until you receive an individual text message inviting you back."

Throughout the day, group text messages from Janie and others flooded my phone. At 3:34 p.m., Janie felt led to send me a personal text message saying, "Chuck's blood pressure is dropping. They called Mary Ellen back to see him and make the decision for DNR." At 3:36 p.m. I texted Janie back, "I'm on my way."

Chuck passed away right before I walked into his hospital room. The situation was very surreal as I watched the nurse unhook the breathing machine from Chuck. Silently, I began praying, "Lord, why did you bring me back to the hospital now. What am I supposed to do? Should I wait until everyone in the room leaves and lay hands on him again?"

As I stared at Chuck's motionless face, the Lord spoke a thought impression into my mind which enabled me to connect the spiritual dots between the time Chuck had questioned me why he should allow me to live in the RV park and our *free-will* decision each of us makes that determines where we end up spending eternity. I was so grateful for the confirmation that he was indeed with Jesus now.

Six days later, we held Chuck's funeral at the RV park where most of us lived. While I was conducting Chuck's eulogy, it was eerie seeing everything unfold the way it did. All of the questions that I had written six months earlier that are listed in chapter five of this book were answered. If you died tomorrow, would you spend eternity with God and those you love, or would you be separated eternally from God and those you love? If your life ended tomorrow, would anyone really care? What would people say about you at your funeral? How many people do you think would even bother to attend? These questions might seem strange, but my father's death and countless others have caused me to get my own affairs in order.

While I was praying about the eulogy, I had felt led to go to Mary Ellen's Facebook page so that I could review posts that she had made before Chuck got sick. My jaw dropped when I saw the two that she posted on September 2, 2015. The first one was a question which asked, "At your funeral, what kind of music would you want to be played?" The second post was the poem (cited below) which brought great comfort to Mary Ellen later because it is a powerful reminder that Chuck is in heaven. Rather than being separated from her for eternity, they will be together in eternity.

AS I SIT IN HEAVEN

Heaven is truly beautiful
Just you wait and see
So live your life, laugh again,
Enjoy yourself, be free.
Then I know with every breath you take
You'll be taking one for me!!!
~ Author Unknown

Somewhere around fifty to seventy-five family, friends and neighbors came to celebrate Chuck's life. The women's Bible study group that met at our RV park rejoiced, knowing that Chuck had accepted Christ as his Savior before he died.

Four months after Chuck passed away, Randy Fox unexpectedly became very sick and died. He was only fifty-eight-years old. Randy and Janie Fox not only bought my home on Mulberry Way in Cedar Park, but we became friends. A month before Randy died, he read a rough draft of the first edition of this book. Then we sat on his back porch while he grilled me with questions for over an hour. I am so very glad we had that conversation.

We never know when our earthly lives will end, which is why I strongly encourage everyone to make amends with family and friends, restore broken relationships, invest personal time in your relationship with Christ, and get your affairs in order.

Scripture References

And all of this is a gift from God,
who brought us back to himself through Christ.
And God has given us this task of reconciling people to him.
For God was in Christ, reconciling the world to himself,
no longer counting people's sins against them.
And he gave us this wonderful message of reconciliation.
(2 Corinthians 5:18–19)

For this is how God loved the world:
He gave his one and only Son,
so that everyone who believes in him
will not perish, but have eternal life.
God sent his Son into the world not to judge the world,
but to save the world through him.
There is no judgment against anyone who believes in him.
But anyone who does not believe in him
has already been judged for not believing
in God's one and only Son.
(John 3:16–18)

Self-Reflection Questions

Does my life display the fruit of being a witness who represents Christ?

Am I committed to seeking, finding, and carrying out God's will?

Do I have a sense of urgency to share the Good News Gospel with others?

What keeps me from sharing my personal testimony with others?

Meditate on the scripture verses in this chapter. How do they apply to my life?

Chapter 40

Next Stop, Kansas City

*Even the sparrow finds a home, and the swallow builds her nest
and raises her young at a place near your altar,
O LORD of Heaven's Armies, my King and my God!*
~ Psalm 84:3 ~

One day, while sitting at my computer, a sparrow started literally tapping on the window right next to me. For five straight days, the poor little sparrow kept tapping non-stop on my window all day long. While this was happening, I looked up scripture verses on sparrows, prayed and researched sparrows online but nothing I did released God's revelatory word. Then, on the sixth day, the Lord finally spoke a thought impression into my mind. The Lord said, "If you want to know the meaning of the sparrow, go to Glory House Church today."

I have many fond memories of Glory House Church, having learned a lot about spiritual gifts from there. Since I hadn't been back in seven years, I looked forward to attending church there on Sunday. Upon my arrival, I was surprised to bump into Brett Lee who normally attends a different church. Though he had recently done some graphic artwork for me, I had not seen him in person in years. I mentioned my intent to pay him what was owed him, but Brett assured me that he felt led to contribute his service to my ministry for free. Praise God!

While we worshiped, I thanked God for Brett's love offering. Then my prayers shifted and I found myself asking, "Lord, what is the meaning of the sparrow? Why did you keep that tiny little bird tapping on my window nonstop?" During worship, corporate prophetic words flowed through the pastoral leadership team. Afterward, Mark Henderson's sermon aligned with the nightly text message that I've been sending myself on God's behalf.

The message from God was, "Do you love me?" Then it reads, "The world has yet to see what God can do with, and for, and through, and in a man, who is fully and wholly consecrated to Him." Right before Mark ended his sermon, he posted a slide of a sparrow, with the following scripture.

"Seek the Kingdom of God above all else,
and live righteously, and THEN God will
give you everything you need."
(Matthew 6:33)

The Lord had set the time and given me the grace to write two books between 2015 and 2018. Minutes after I uploaded my second book, Angie Presley and Mary Ellen Foster informed me that Camper Resort was closing indefinitely. The park had been flooded in October 2018, just months after I moved, and the entire septic system needed replacement, along with other extensive repairs.

I needed to move, but at this point didn't have a clue to where. Then Laura Berndt contacted me and invited me to attend Immerse, an eight-day training program at IHOPKC in Kansas City. Since I'd been to IHOPKC before, I knew it would be a nice spiritual retreat, but I also sensed that God might be relocating me there, which added to my excitement about going. Laura lined up accommodations for both Wade Ferris and me, and he graciously covered the cost of the event, which made it possible for me to go.

I picked up Wade and we started on the twelve-hour trip. Unfortunately, my transmission gave out in Waco, Texas. After a tow to a local dealership, they offered me a free car until I told them that we were heading across state lines to Missouri. Then we learned it would cost us $500 to rent a car for a week. I found myself facing yet another *crisis of belief*. Since I couldn't afford $500, I prayed silently that Wade would pull out his credit card to pay for the rental if it was the Lord's will for us to press on. When Wade did, I knew the Lord wanted us to persevere.

The eight-day Immerse was impactful, especially for people being led towards the narrow path that few find and fewer follow. During the week, I used our breaks to look into and count the cost of what it would take to relocate to Grandview, Missouri. I also prayed throughout the week about selling my fifth wheel so that I could raise money to keep serving in ministry full-time. I've learned that selling things when needed is simply part of living a lifestyle of faith.

While driving around Kansas City, Missouri, throughout the week, Wade and I started noticing the number 33 appearing everywhere. It happened so many times we kept laughing every time we saw the number 33. When I got back to Austin, I called Don Vaughn, the salesman who had sold me my RV. When I asked him what my RV was worth, he said, "$33,000," which was another confirmation that the Lord wanted me to sell and move to IHOPKC.

I got the RV ready to sell and posted it on my Facebook page. As I was posting the ads on RV Trader, Craigslist, and five RV trading Facebook sites, Mary Ellen and Angie went to lunch for the first time with Ken Bjork, a member of their church. They were surprised when out of the blue he said, "I am thinking of buying an RV." After lunch, Ken came over to check it out. After looking at it, he said he was interested in buying it, but then it appeared that he lost interest since I didn't hear from him for weeks.

While praying about what to do, the Lord told me to do the opposite of what common sense dictates. Rather than posting my RV for sale on many sites, the Lord told me to take down the one posting that I had made. The Lord said, "If you want to get the full $33,000, wait on Ken to buy it, and trust my perfect timing." Rather than advertise my RV, I found myself practicing patience and exercising faith once more. While I was waiting on Ken, I sold a few things and gave away everything else I owned including a storage unit full of food that Pastor George Crisp gladly picked up to feed four orphanages in Mexico.

Ken finally called and offered to buy my RV for exactly $33,000. Shortly thereafter, a company I used to work for informed me of pension money coming which I didn't even know I had and that it was available immediately. Between both, I've been able to relocate to IHOPKC to continue serving Christ full-time.

Within a week of my relocation, I was invited to serve on the Forerunner Church prayer altar ministry team and attend a prophetic ministry activation class. Since it had been eight years since I had served on a prophetic ministry team, I decided to go to the IHOPKC Global Prayer Room to seek confirmation before attending the meeting that night. As soon as I got out of my car, I saw Brent Smallwood coming out of the Global Prayer Room. I hadn't seen or talked to Brent, who still lives near Springfield since I had served on his prophetic ministry team eight years ago. Wow! Talk about God's perfect timing. Clearly, the Lord wanted me to get back into the prophetic flow. Praise God!

It was great seeing Brent again, though a great loss had led him to spend an entire week at IHOPKC seeking the Father's heart in the GPR. During his time here, I got to share my brotherly love for him as we worked together as a prophetic ministry team as we often did in Springfield.

While writing this revised and updated edition, I currently volunteer on IHOPKC prophetic ministry teams, the Forerunner Church prayer altar ministry team, and as a leader of a Doing Family Together Friendship

Group that meets in my apartment on Sunday nights. I also spend an exorbitant amount of time trying to reach, teach, correct, and inspire the 4,600 people who are connected to me through my Facebook page.

For the past sixteen plus years, I've served full-time in ministry without any personal support or compensation. While discussing funding with a mature believer who wrote a wonderful endorsement of my first book, he asked me, "Do you really expect others to be as committed to pursuing Christ as you are?" I replied, "My job is to do the will of Him who called and sent me to do His work. In order to do that, I focus on pleasing an audience of One."

Scripture References

We must endure many hardships to enter the kingdom of God.
(Acts 14:23)

If it seems we are crazy, it is to bring glory to God.
And if we are in our right minds, it is for your benefit.
Either way, Christ's love controls us.
Since we believe that Christ died for all,
we also believe that we have all died to our old life.
He died for everyone so that those who receive his new life
will no longer live for themselves.
(2 Corinthians 5:13–15)

After preaching the Good News in Derbe
and making many disciples,
Paul and Barnabas returned to
Lystra, Iconium, and Antioch of Pisidia,
where they strengthened the believers.
They encouraged them to continue in the faith,
reminding them that we must suffer many hardships
to enter the Kingdom of God.
(Acts 14:21–22)

For when we brought you the Good News,
it was not only with words but also with power,
for the Holy Spirit gave you full assurance that what we said was true.
And you know of our concern for you
from the way we lived when we were with you.
(1 Thessalonians 1:5)

Self-Reflection Questions

Am I seeking the Kingdom above all my other priorities?

What adjustments do I need to make to live righteously?

Am I hearing and following Jesus, or my own carnal thoughts?

Is my life centered around pleasing God, or the cares of this world, people, and things that will soon perish?

Meditate on the scripture verses in this chapter.
How do they apply to my life?

Eternal Salvation Prayer

Have you asked Jesus to make a home in your heart? If not now, when? If you have read this far, it's not an accident. It's a divine appointment!

God's word tells us in Romans 10:4, "For Christ has already accomplished the purpose for which the law was given. As a result, all who believe in him are made right with God."

When you receive Jesus as your Lord and Savior, you become a child of God. He delivers you from the kingdom of darkness and by his power you enter into the Kingdom of Light. It is this *free-will* decision that activates His divine intervention. In Christ, you are justified. He sees you just as though you have never sinned. It is by Christ's righteousness that we are made right with our Heavenly Father, not self-righteousness. A person is saved by faith not by works so that no man can boast. We don't do good things in order to be saved; we do good things because we are saved. (Read John 1:12; Colossians 1:13-14; Romans 5:9-11; 1 Corinthians 15:3-4; Ephesians 2:8-9).

His word continues to tell us in Romans 10:9-13, "If you openly declare that Jesus is Lord and believe in your heart that God raised him from the dead, you will be saved. For it is by believing in your heart that you are made right with God, and it is by openly declaring your faith that you are saved.

As the Scriptures tell us, "Anyone who trusts in him will never be disgraced." Jew and Gentile are the same in this respect. They have the same Lord, who gives generously to all who call on him. For "Everyone who calls on the name of the Lord will be saved."

Your words don't have to be perfect, He just wants to hear you speak from your heart. Here's how simple it is to receive His amazing grace.

Pray something like this:

> **Heavenly Father,**
>
> Thank you for sending your son Jesus to die on the cross for my sins and for raising Him from the dead so that I could have Life. I ask that you forgive me for all of my sins.
> I invite your son Jesus to make a home in my heart and to fill me with your Holy Spirit so that I can understand spiritual truths and be born again. Thank you for forgiving me. I am now a new creation in Christ Jesus.
>
> **It is in Jesus' name that I pray, Amen.**

If you have made this decision to ask Christ Jesus into your heart and confessed with your mouth that Jesus is Lord and Savior, congratulations! Welcome to God's family!

I encourage you to read your Bible, pray, and find a Bible-believing church to fellowship with people who are like-minded and desire to pursue and follow Christ. Remember, praying is just talking with God like you would your best friend!

Reviews from the First Edition

A fascinating, compelling book . . . just WOW! It rekindled my passion for Yeshua in a big way. This is a great tool to reach and help disciple others.

~ Kelly Land

Fantastic book! I would have read this in one sitting, but I am 82 years old so it took me two! James' testimony is powerful and is sure to impact many!

~ Della Berndt

James' very transparent autobiography rekindled my "first love experience." Everyone can benefit from this modern-day version of *Pilgrim's Progress* which teaches others how to follow "thought impressions" that lead us into an eternal lifestyle.

~ Nila Campbell

Amazing and inspirational! A true example of what it means to be a disciple of Christ. From the pit of hell to the throne room of God, James' journey is an example of what a loving God can do when we step out in faith and die to ourselves.

~ Pari Rossi

I've watched James transform from a "me" person into a remarkable witness for the Lord. I've witnessed him cashing in everything that he owned and placing it into the Lord's hands. I've told others about some of the miracles which are now documented in this book. I've seen James work tirelessly to lead others to Christ. Praise the Lord!

~ Todd Hindman

I've known James since the first Power of the Cross Festival in 2006 and labored with him for the 2007 event. Rarely will you read a "rawthentic" story of someone's unwavering faith to pursue God's calling on his life. No matter how committed you are to your faith, you will find James' testimony captivating, and further evidence that God's grace can transform your life when you are willing to count worldly possessions as loss for the sake of gaining Christ.

~ Barclay Garman

When James decided to get out of the world's rat race, he was a broken man who needed help. Now he is happy and "running the race God has marked out for him." His story inspires others to trust God to bring change to their lives.

~ *Carolyn Parsons*

The hand of the Father is clearly evident in the life-changing reality of James' personal testimony. His amazing journey documents the transition from selfishness to selflessness. It records the transformation that takes place when we take our eyes off our problems and put them upon the solution, Jesus Christ, who is the author and finisher of our faith. When James made Jesus his number one priority, he discovered that without Christ life wasn't worth living.

~ *Debbie Hechelte*

When I received your book *Crisis of Belief*, I couldn't put it down for eight hours. It was a hard read for me personally as I have been through similar life experiences. Your depth of transparency is a gift. I am often quoted as saying, "Intimacy means in-to-me-you-see." James has allowed us as readers to become very intimate with him through his book. Anyone who has had the pain and hardships that life can often bring will be beyond blessed by James' story. I pray blessings over you, James, and all whose lives you bless in your ministry.

~ *Linda Reinek*

Upon finishing James' autobiography, I was filled with a sense of great peace. If you are a believer, your faith and trust in our Lord will be strengthened and deepened as you read this book. You will be reminded of all God has done in your life, just as He's done in James' life. If you are a seeker or a new believer, rest assured that the same Jesus who, time after time, heard James' fervent prayers is your Savior, too. The Lord came alongside James, spoke to him, comforted him, set up those divine appointments, and provided the grace and mercy James needed in every situation. That's the God we serve! As we go through life we may not get it perfect, but the good news, as James can attest, is that God can cause all things to work for the good. He just needs to have our heart. Thank you, James, for being so open and honest with your story.

~ *Cary Martin*

Love Offering
to
Support this Ministry

As you know, it takes monetary support as well as prayers to advance the Gospel. Your donation of any amount will help me advance this work and continue to do the other things for which I am called.

100% of the site's donations are used to purchases print copies whole-sale. Because of donations, my co-laborers and I have been able to sow free print copies into others' lives. So far, we've given out over 2,000 free print copies of *Crisis of Belief* to individuals and ministries. Over 600 people have downloaded the free digital copy! Praise the Lord!

Thank you for your prayers, any contributions, and any time given to share this message with others. Your gift is helping to reach the lost. May God bless you richly for your generous support.

May the Lord bless and multiply your love offering contribution which enables us to advance the Kingdom!

Blessings,

James Timothy Butt

About the Author

James is a forerunner for Christ and a trailblazer for our generation. Like King David, he is "A Man After God's Own Heart."

The Lord separated James on April 5th, 2003 to become a special witness to verify God's amazing grace and truth. Everything that defined James perception of himself was stripped away. Suddenly and passionately, God's calling became an all-consuming fire that began to mold, shape, and redefine the new person that James was becoming. Once he recognized his Savior, he counted the cost, burned his bridges, put his hand to the plow, and by the power of God's grace, James has never looked back. His treasures are now stored up in heaven and his life is hidden in Christ.

James has served with several churches and para-church ministries, and has participated in both Kairos and Bill Glass prison ministries.

He has been apostolically ordained, led hundreds of people to Christ, and has written three books which have been read by thousands.

James continues to spend exorbitant amounts of time and energy discipling people daily through his personal Facebook page that ministers to over four thousand five hundred followers.

Please visit **www.CrisisOfBelief.com** to learn more, or email Jim at: JamesTimothyButt@gmail.com

 Find us on Facebook: James Timothy Butt, and Crisis of Belief.

Made in the USA
Monee, IL
20 March 2021